The Best Alien and UFO Coloring Book

Dr. Melissa Caudle

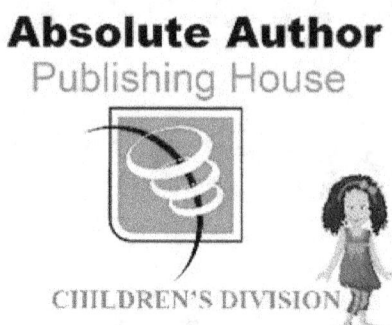

The Best Alien and UFO Coloring Book
Copyright © 2023 by Dr. Melissa Caudle
ALL RIGHTS RESERVED

Publisher: Absolute Author Publishing House
Associate Editor: Kathy Rabb Kittok
Cover Designer and Illustrator: Touhid Wahid

Hardback ISBN: 978-1-64953-714-0
Paperback ISBN: 978-1-64953-715-7

About the Author

Dr. Melissa Caudle is an award-winning retired principal and bestselling author of over 100 books for adults and children.

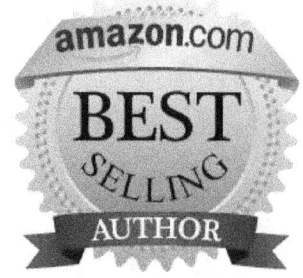

This book belongs to:

_____

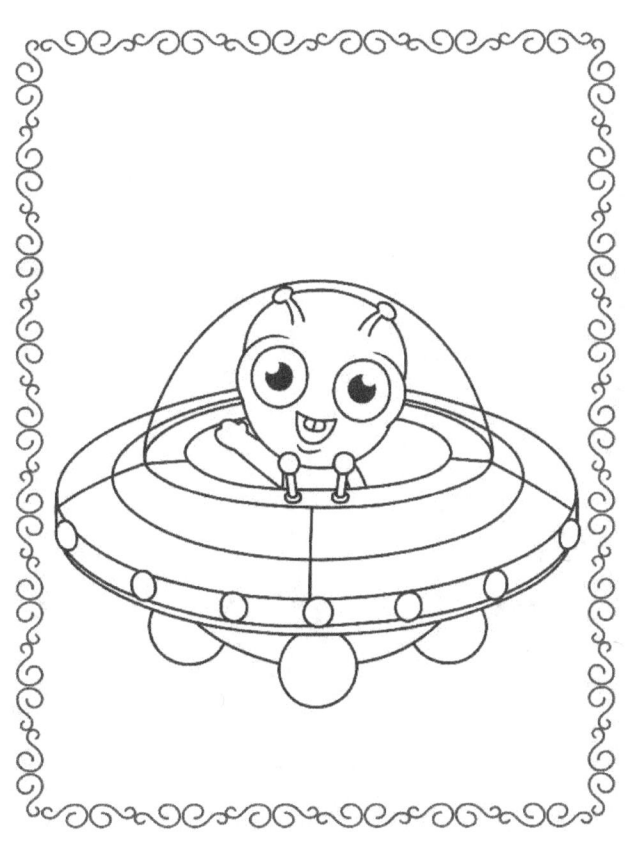

COLOR TEST PAGE

COLOR TEST PAGE

COLOR TEST PAGE

COLOR TEST PAGE

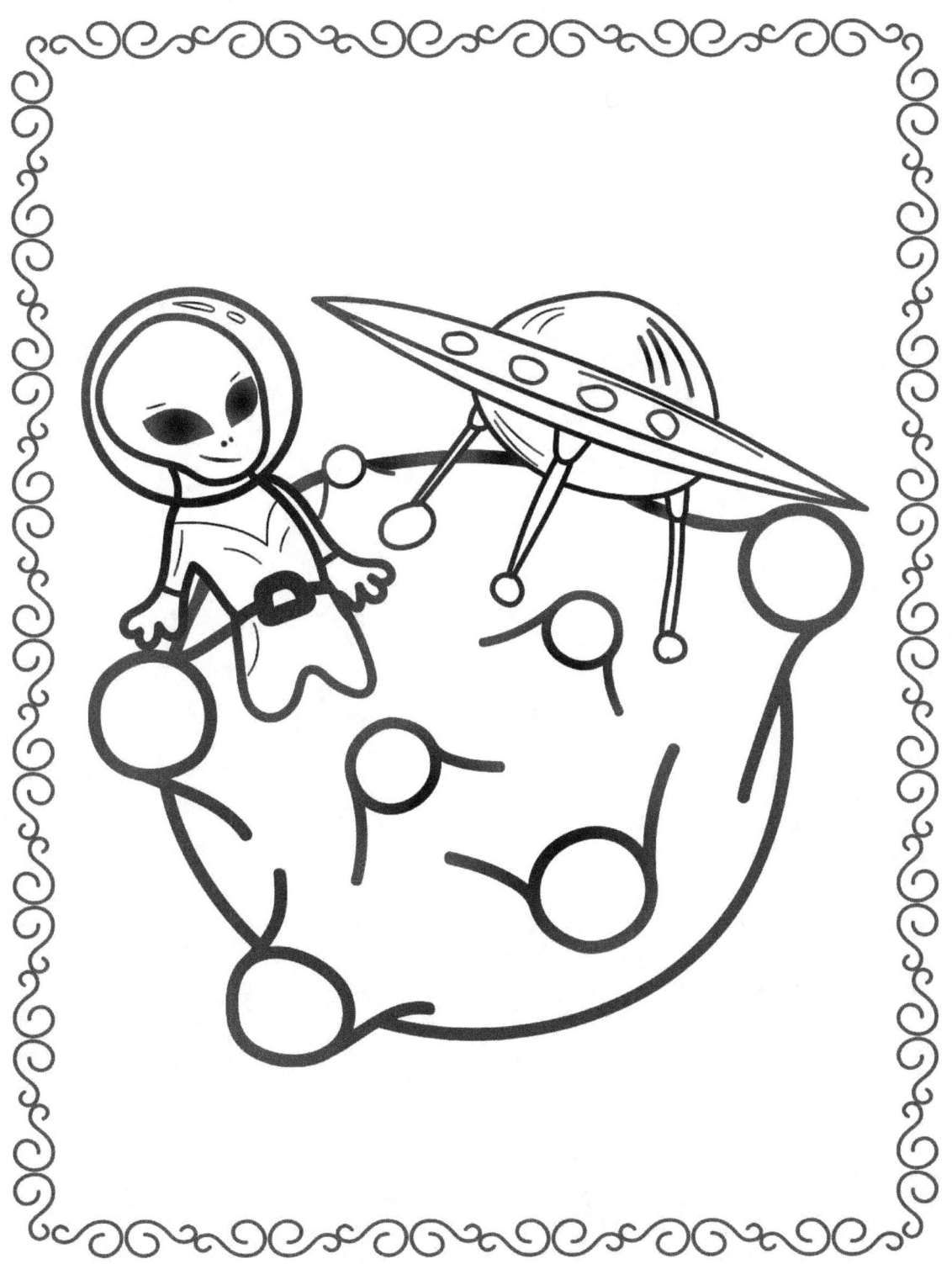

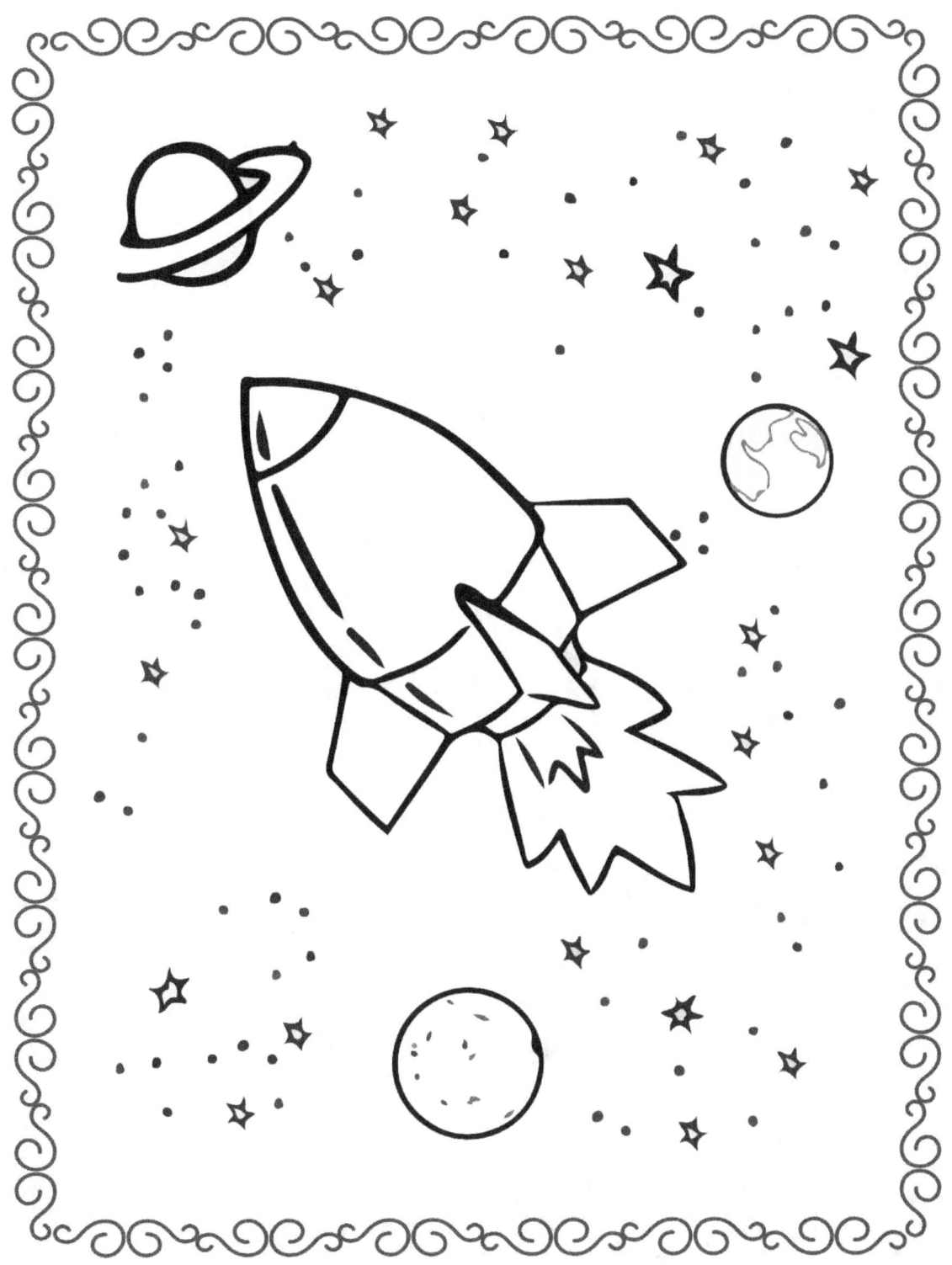

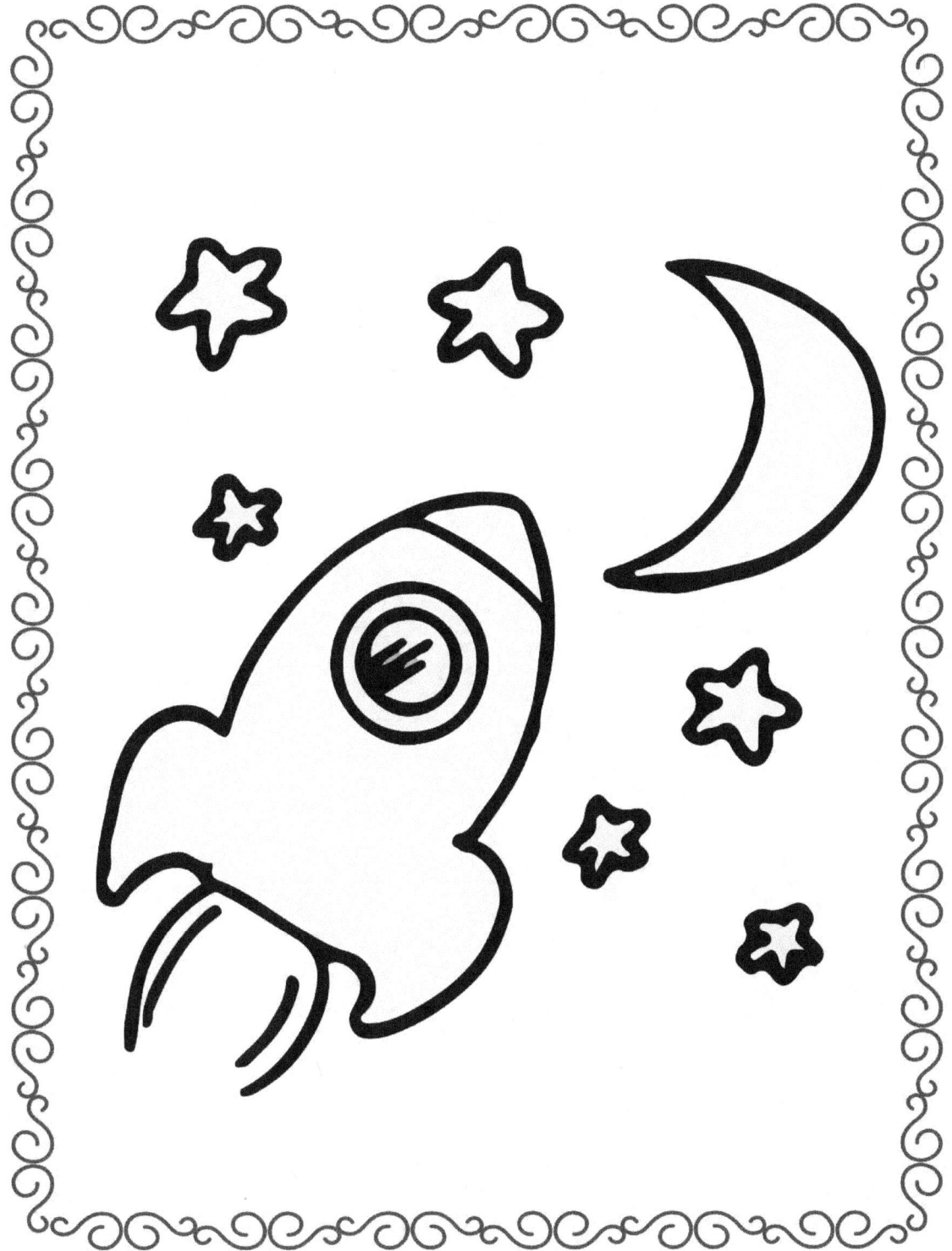

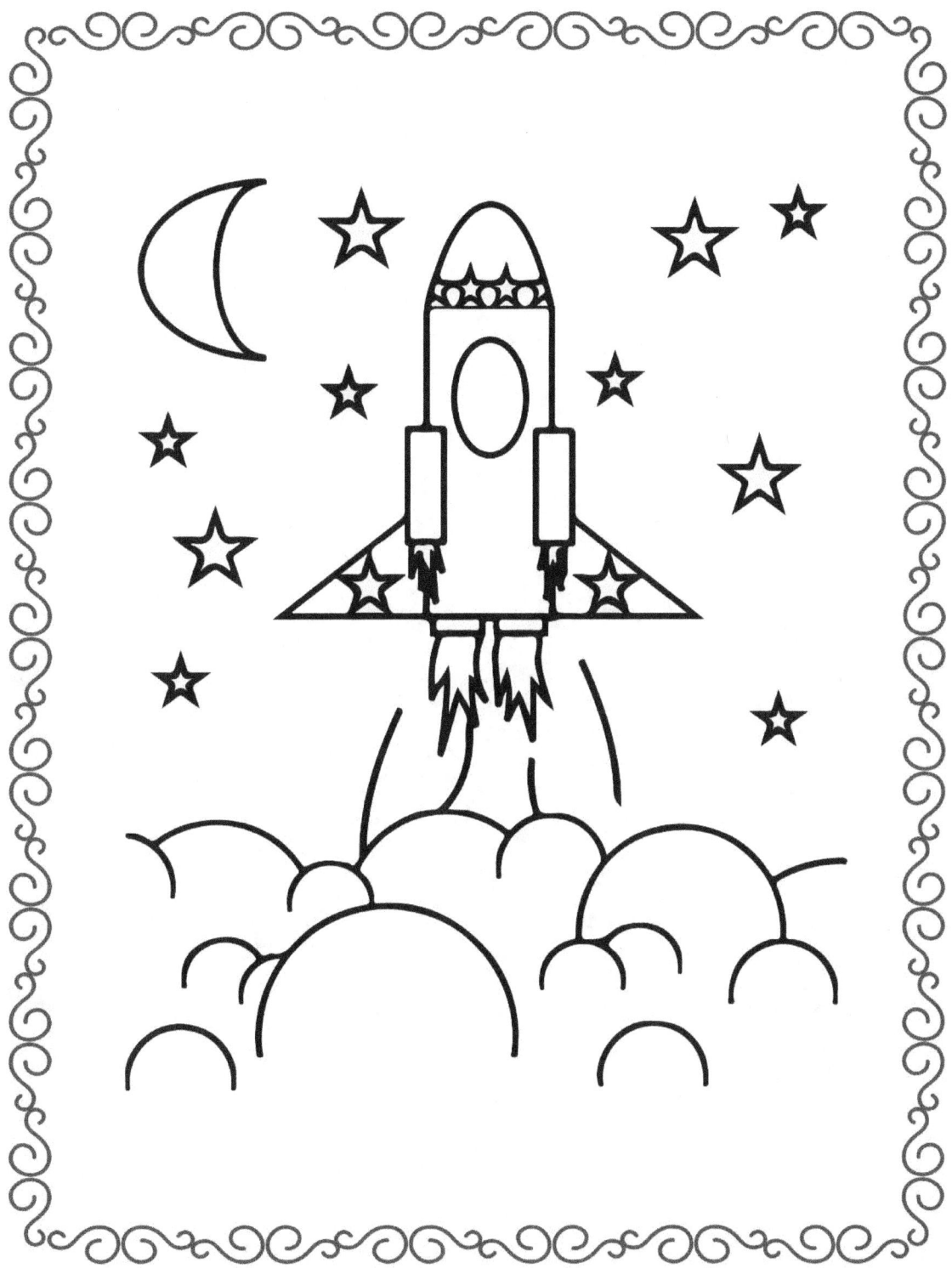

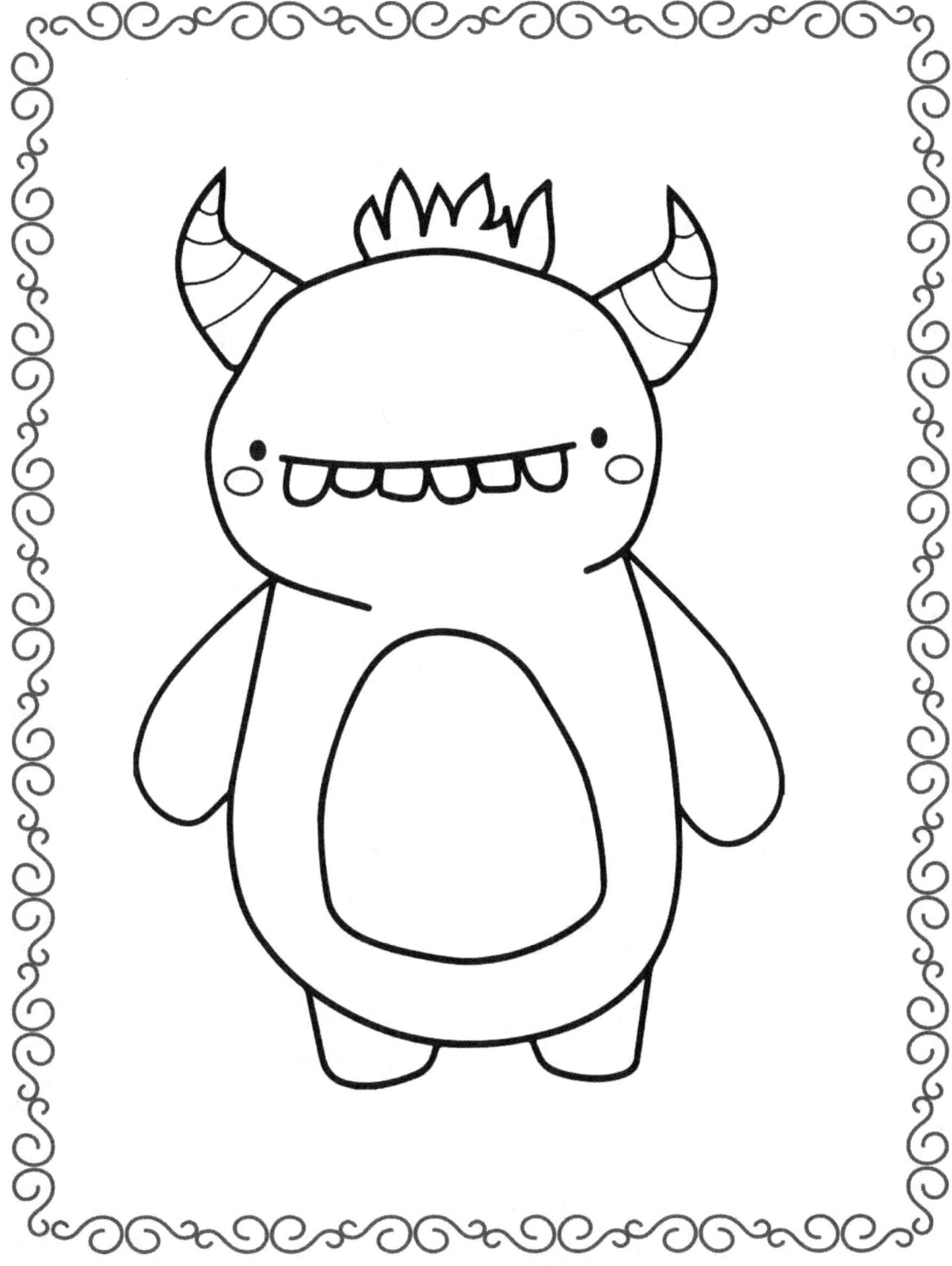

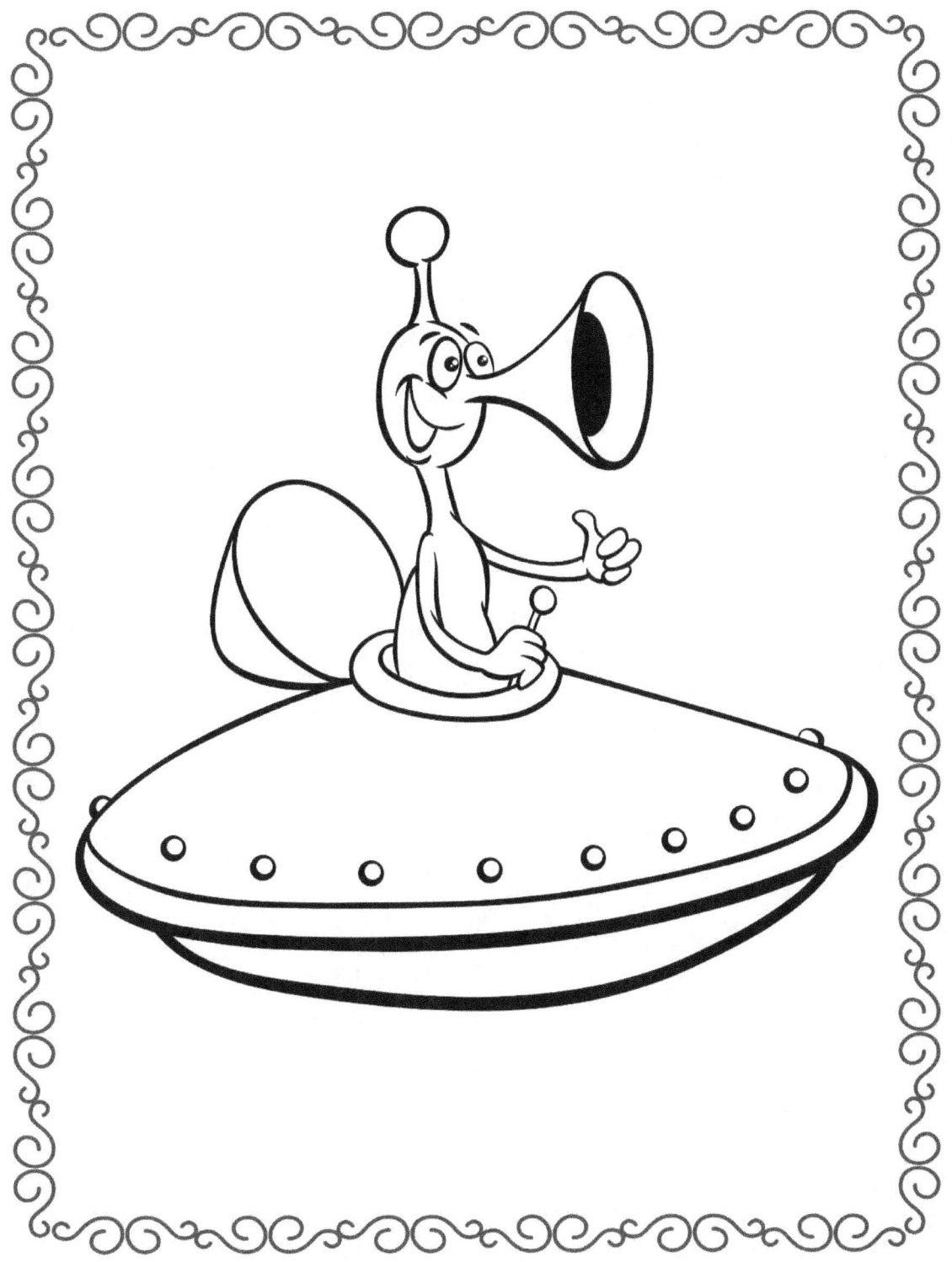

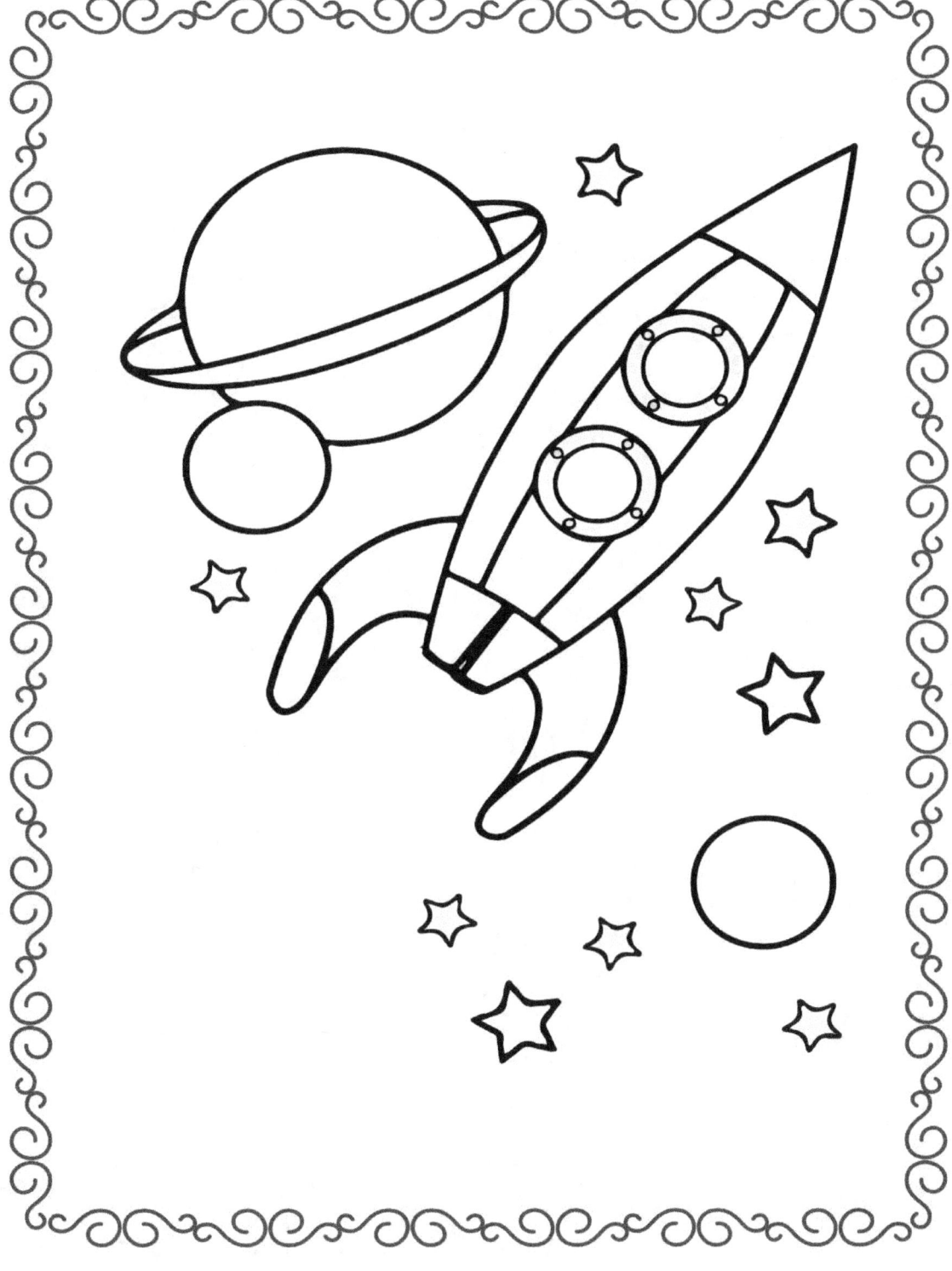

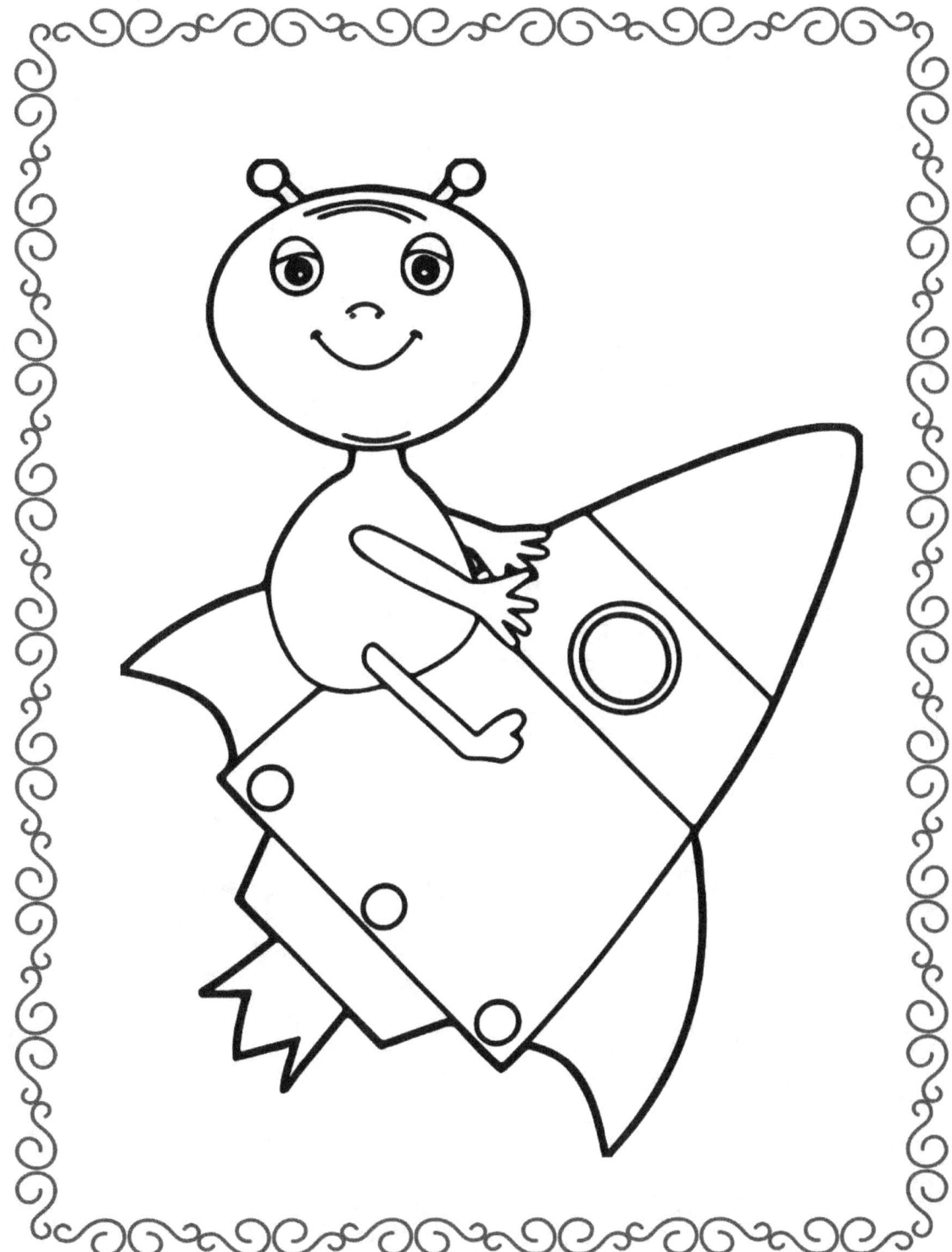

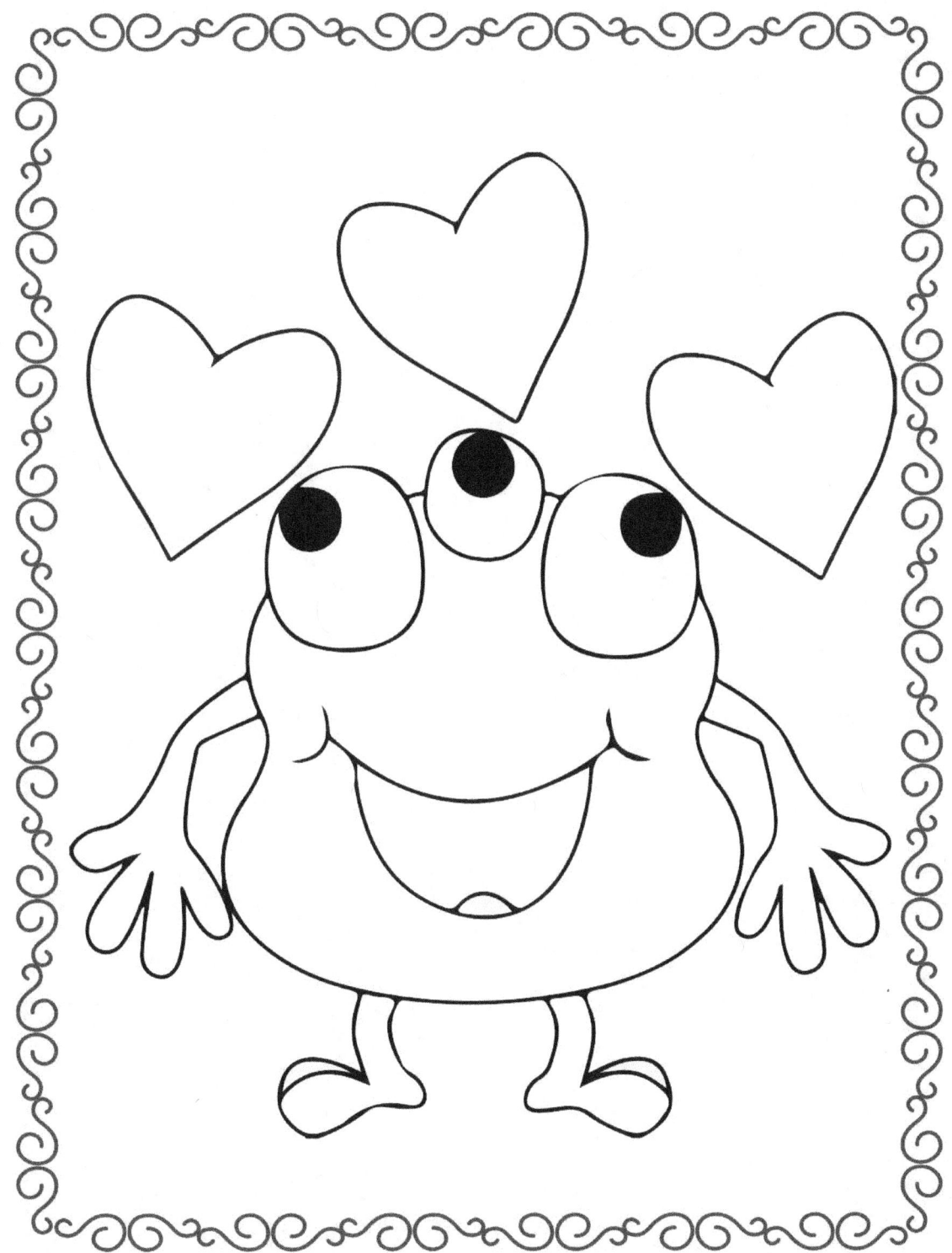

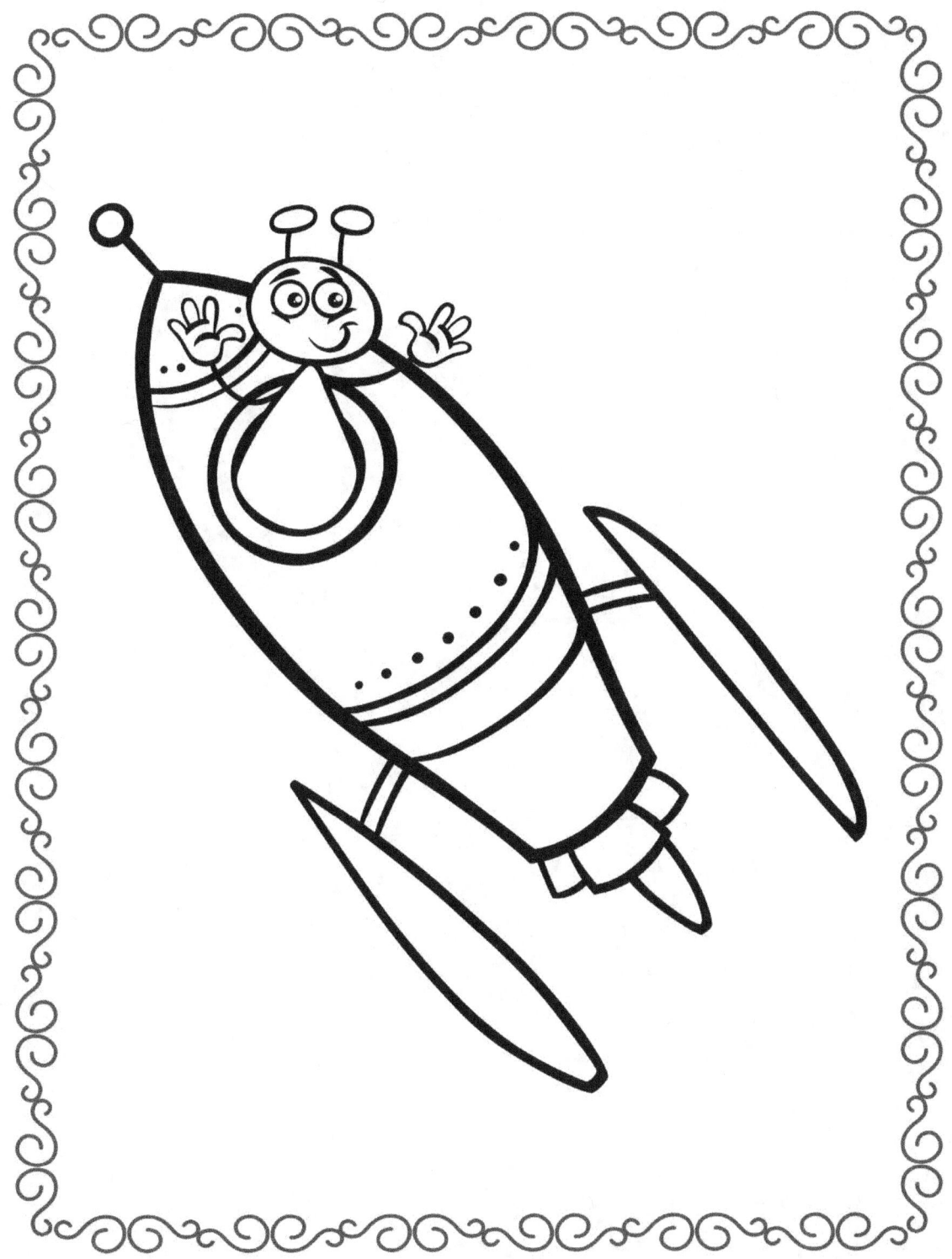

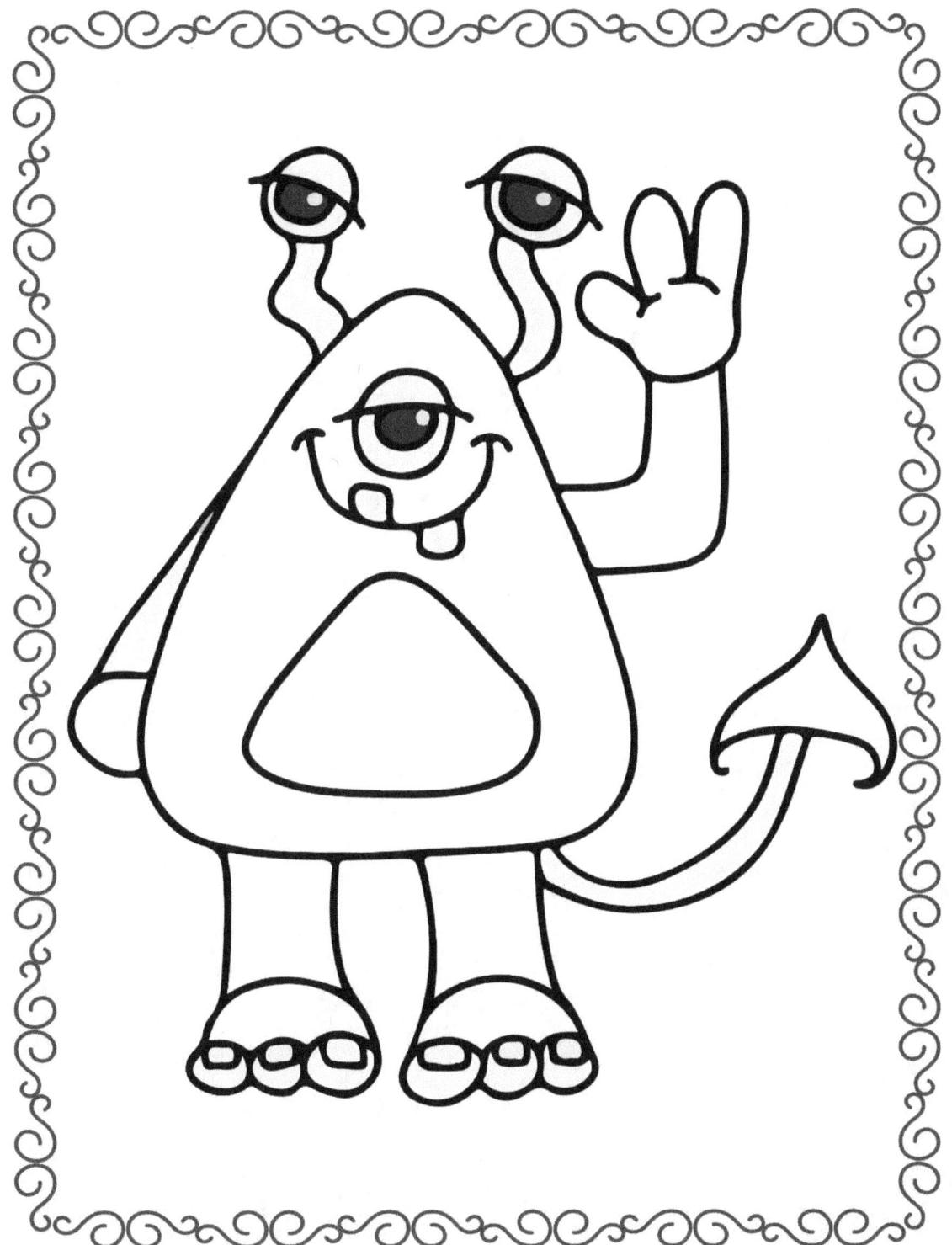

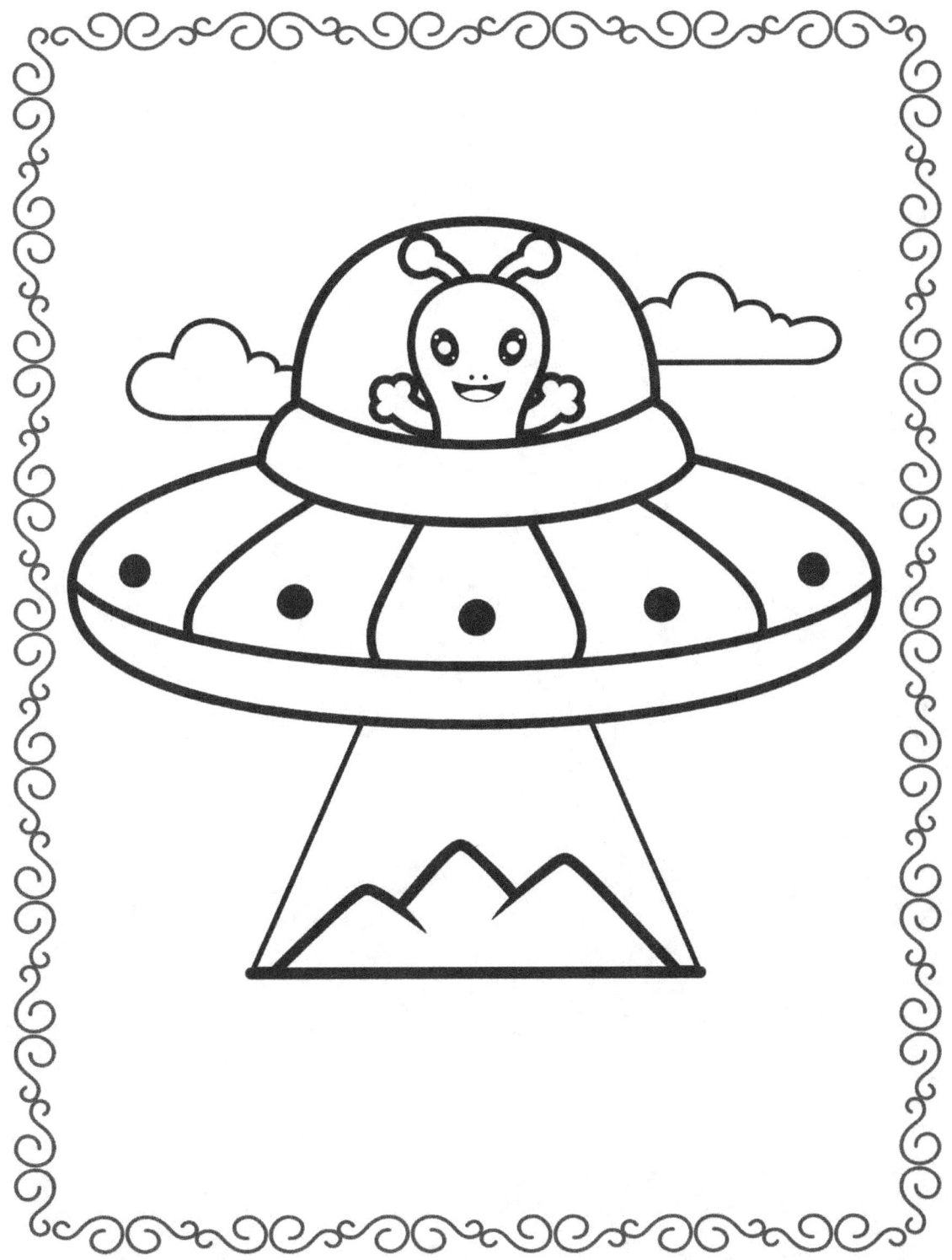

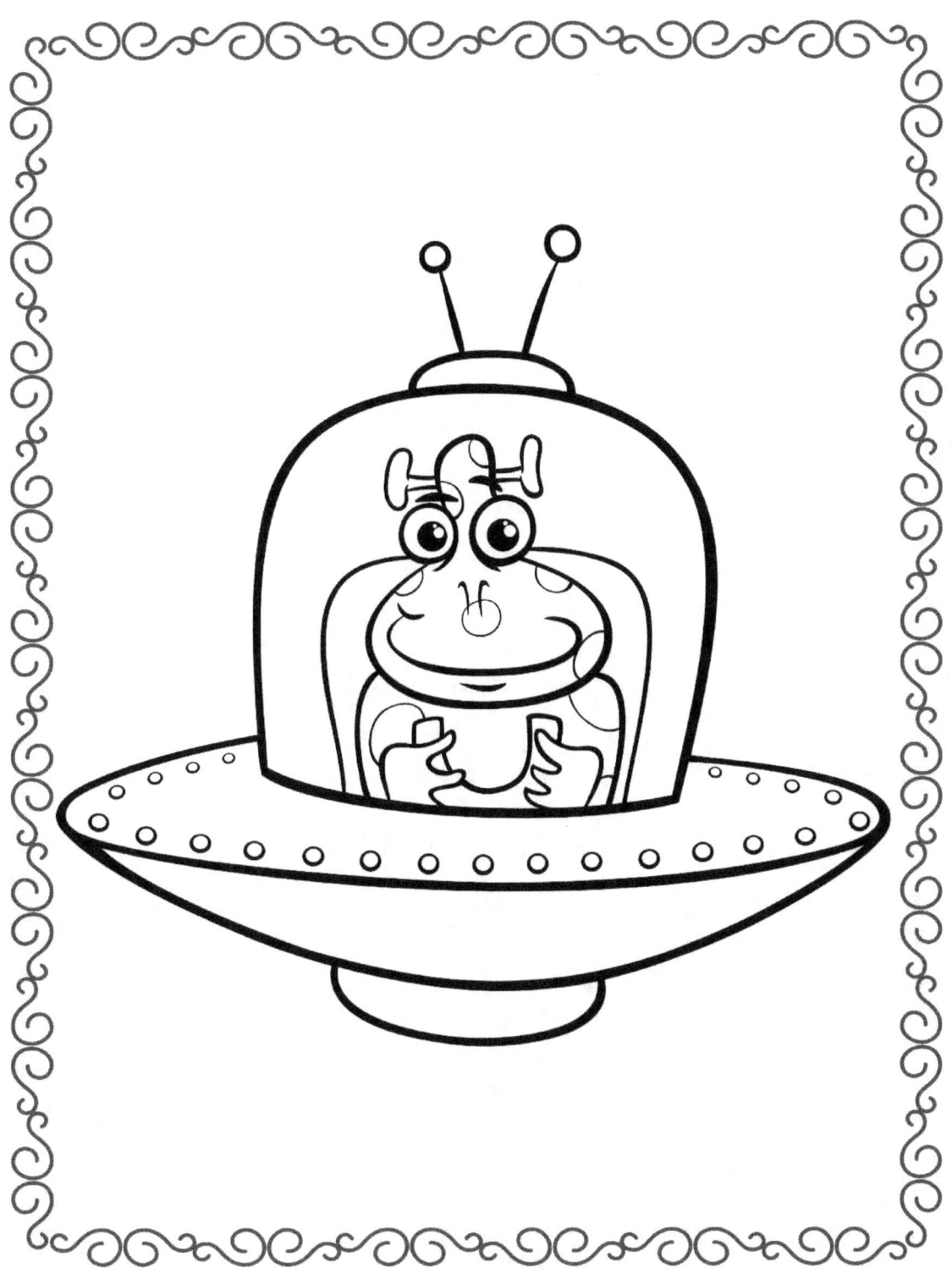

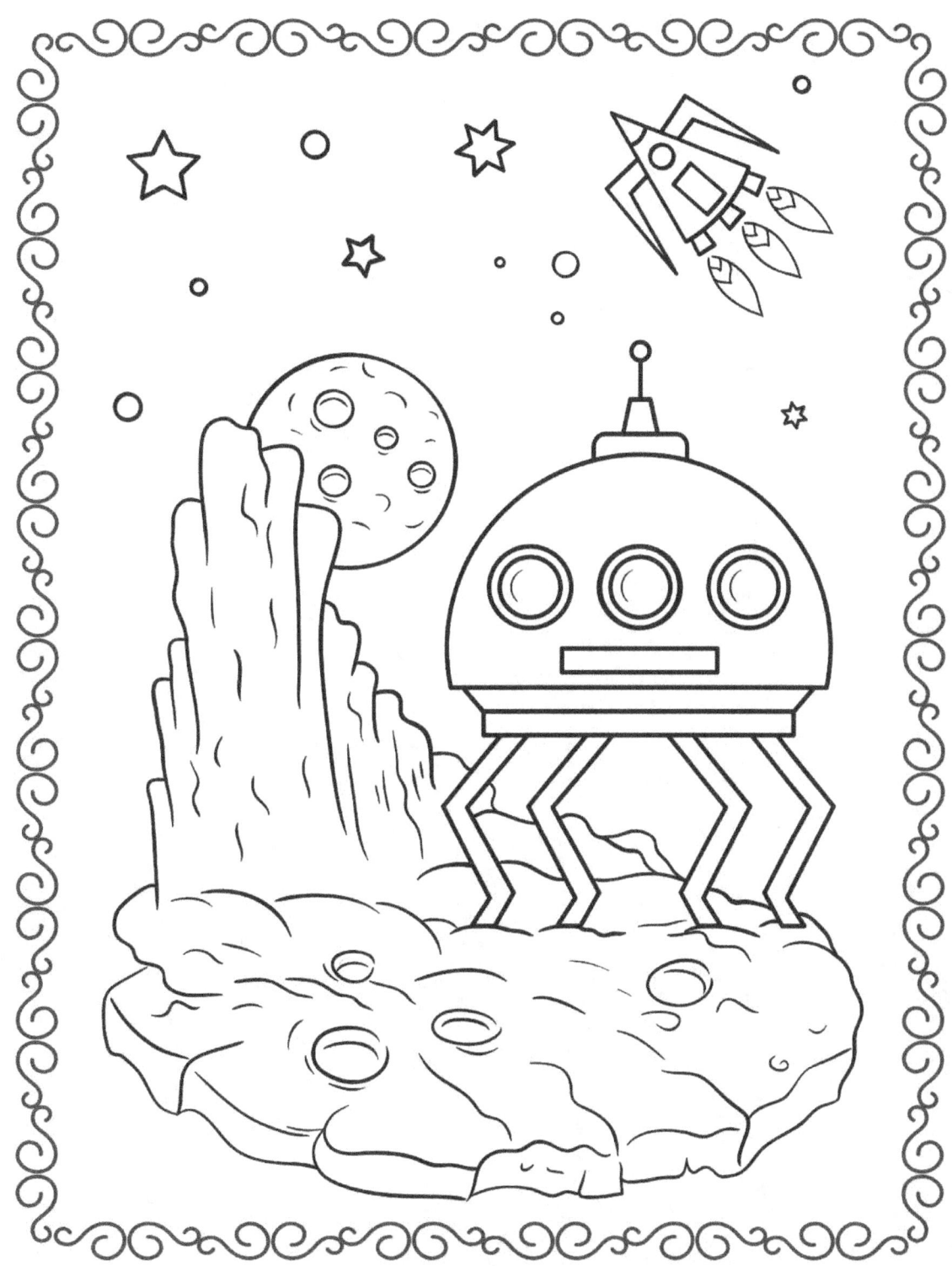

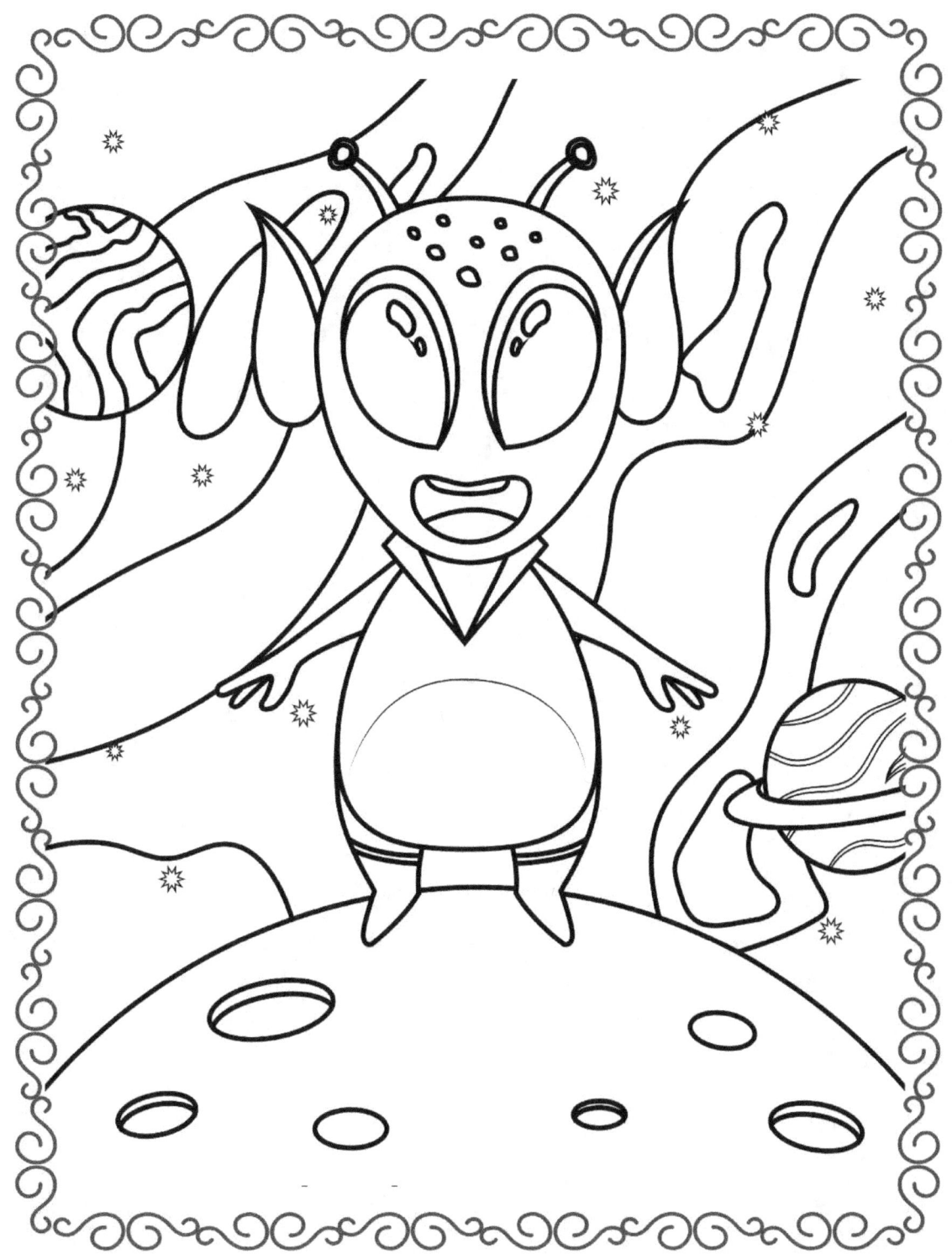

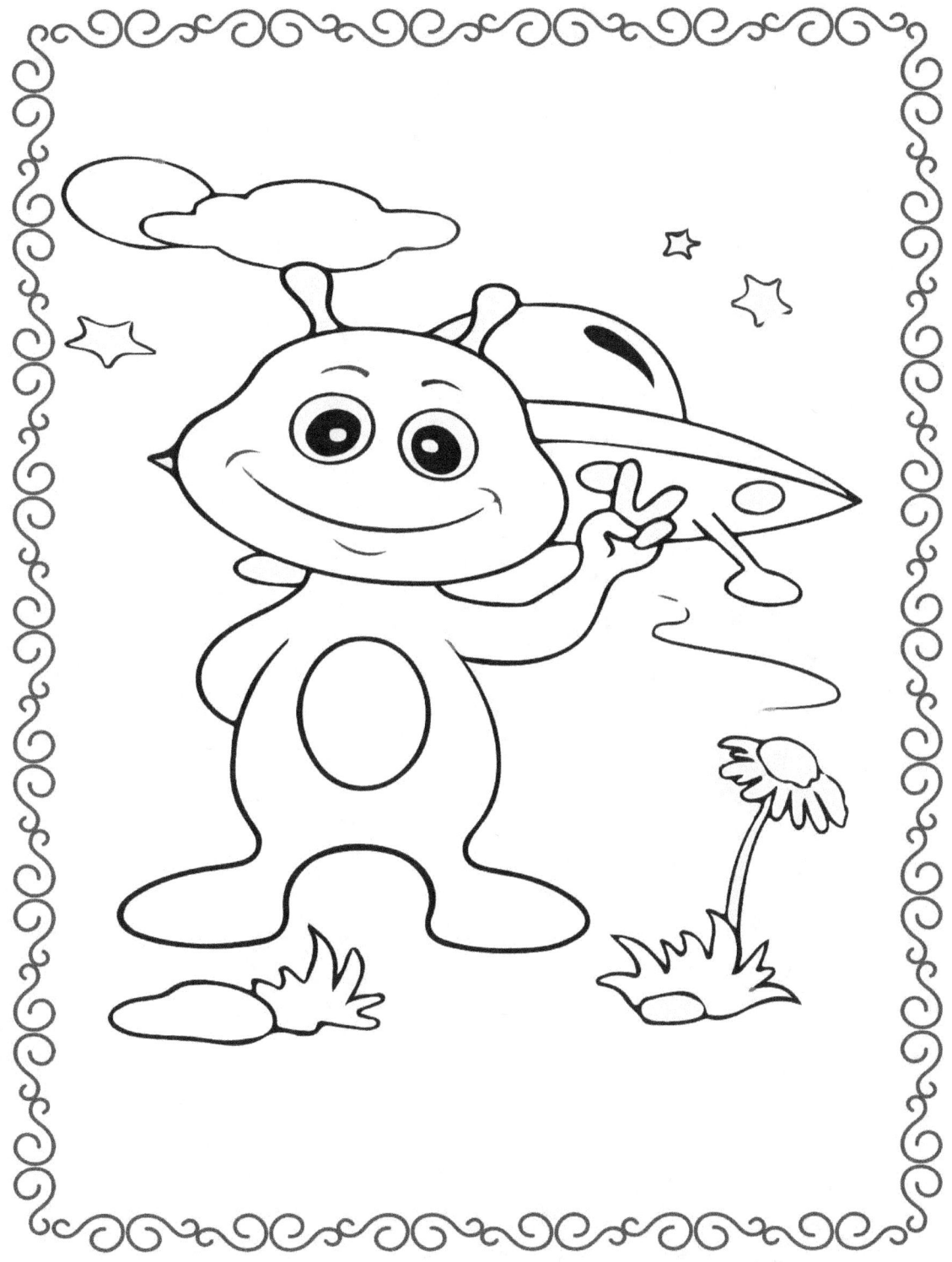

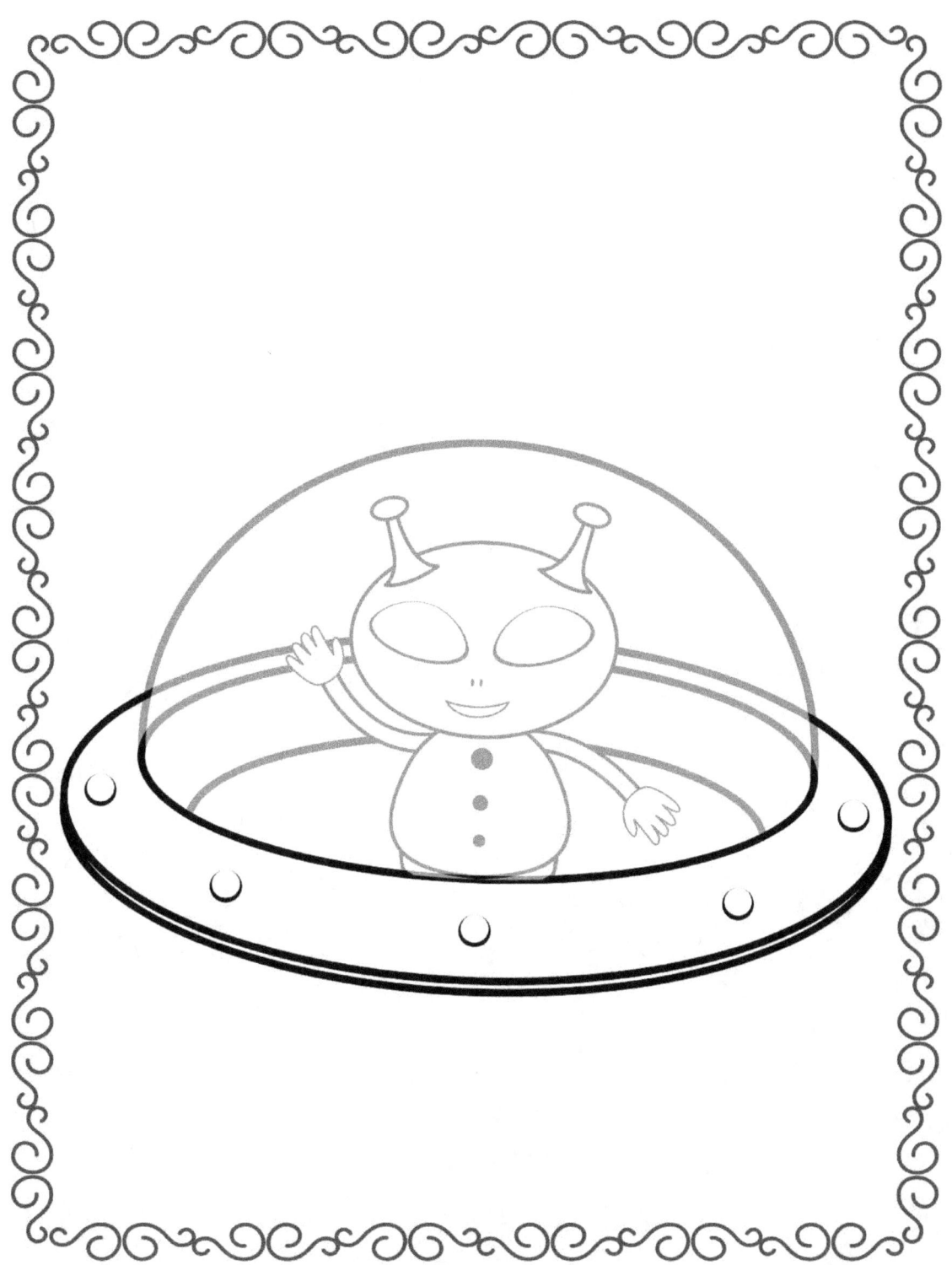

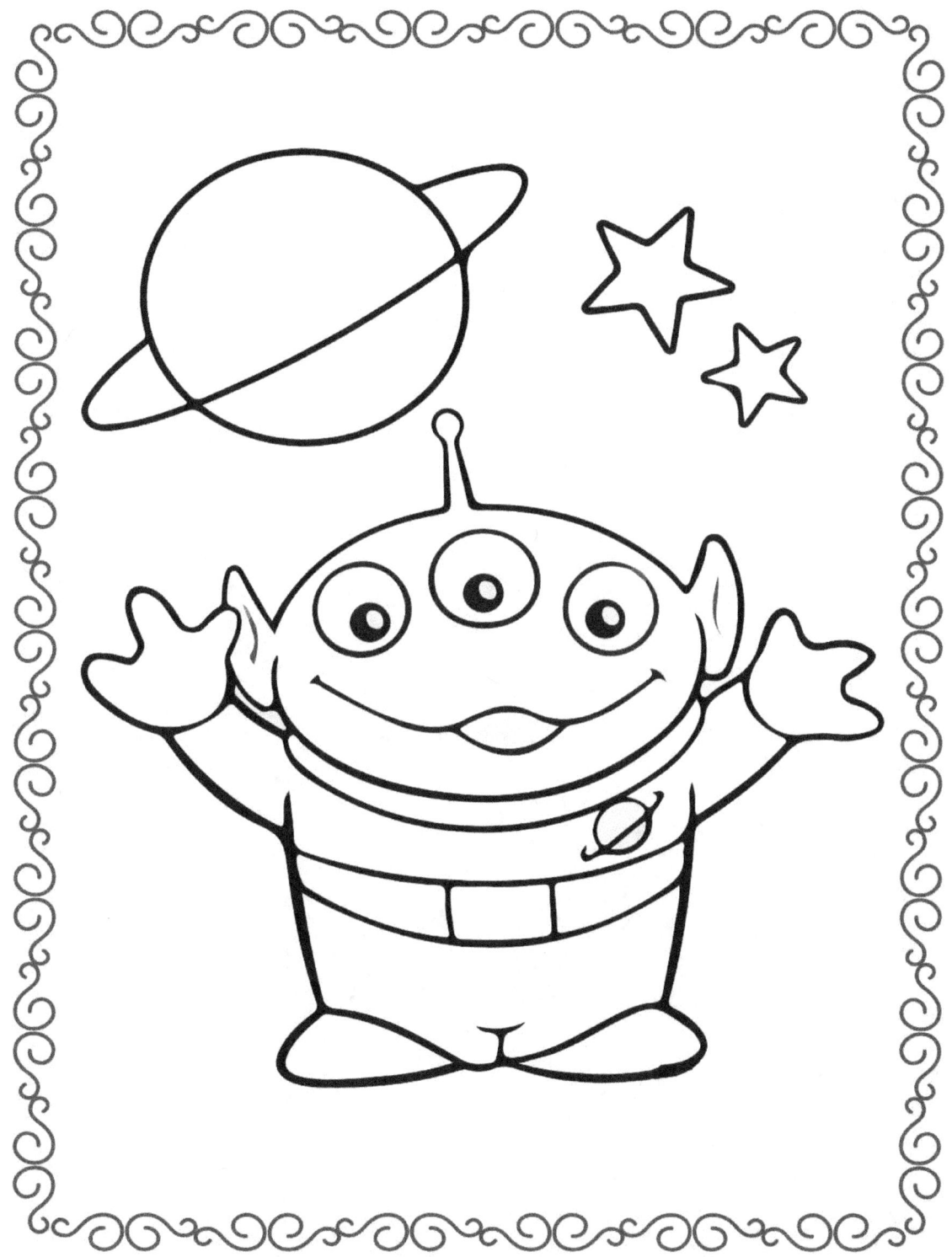

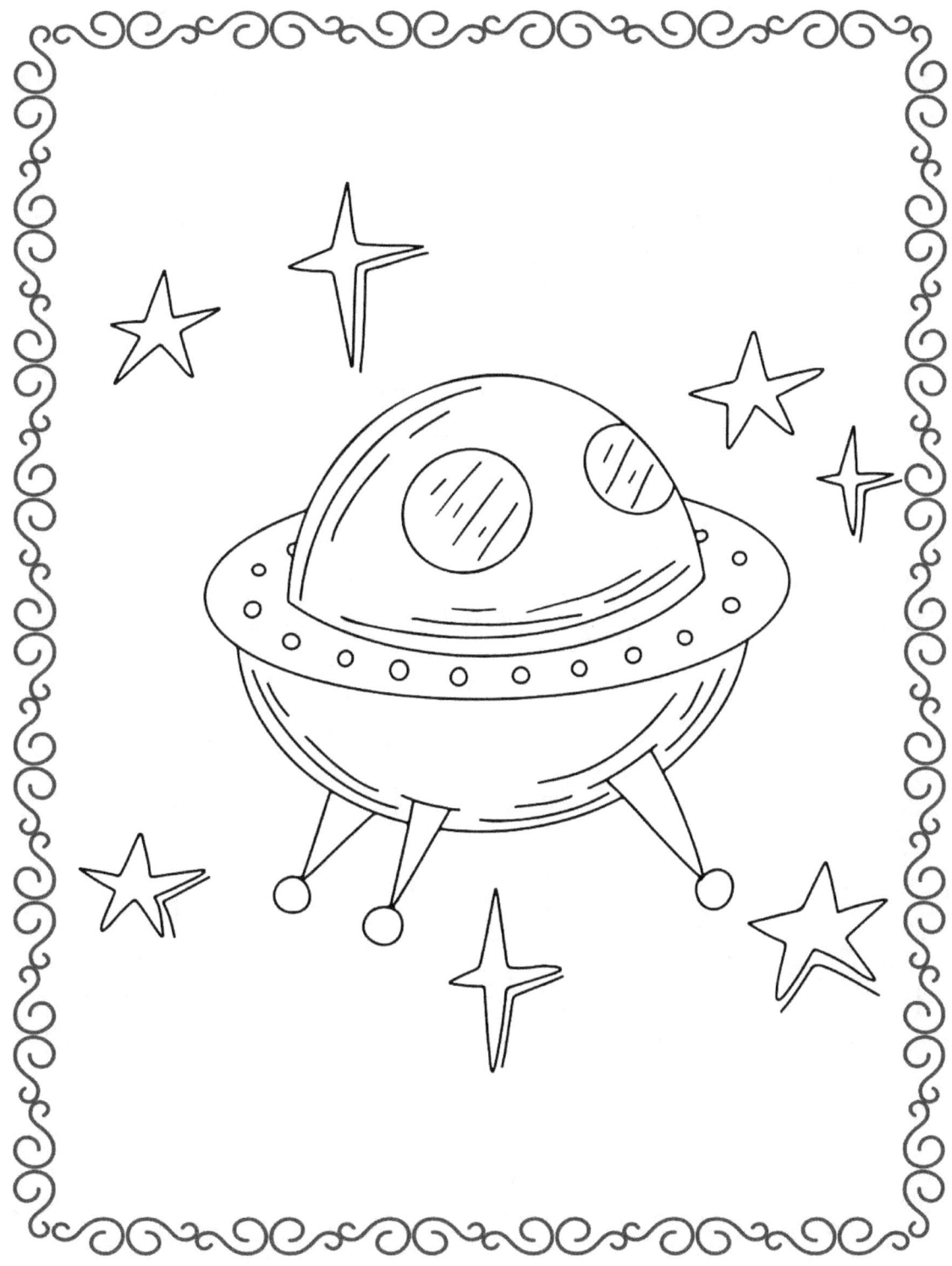

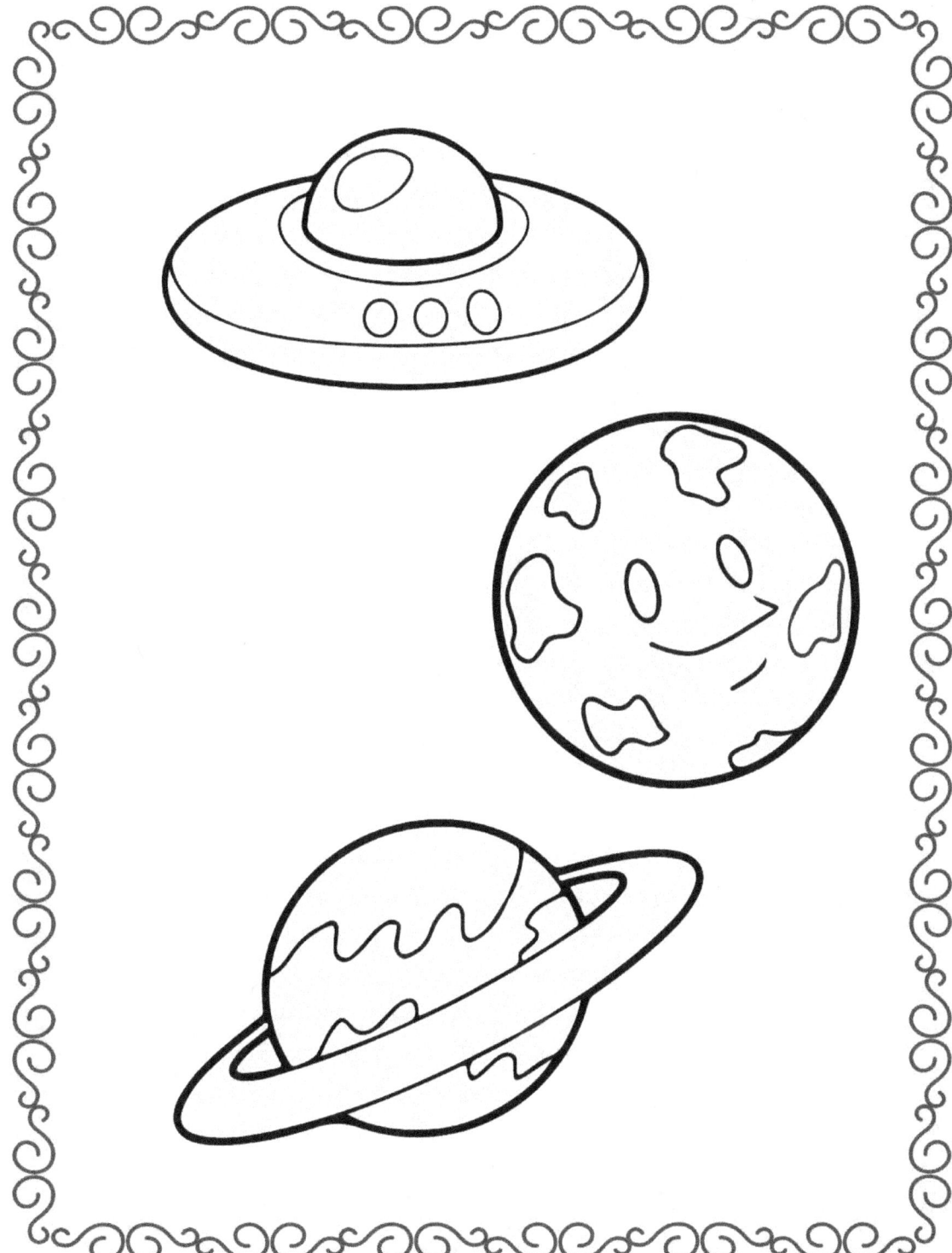

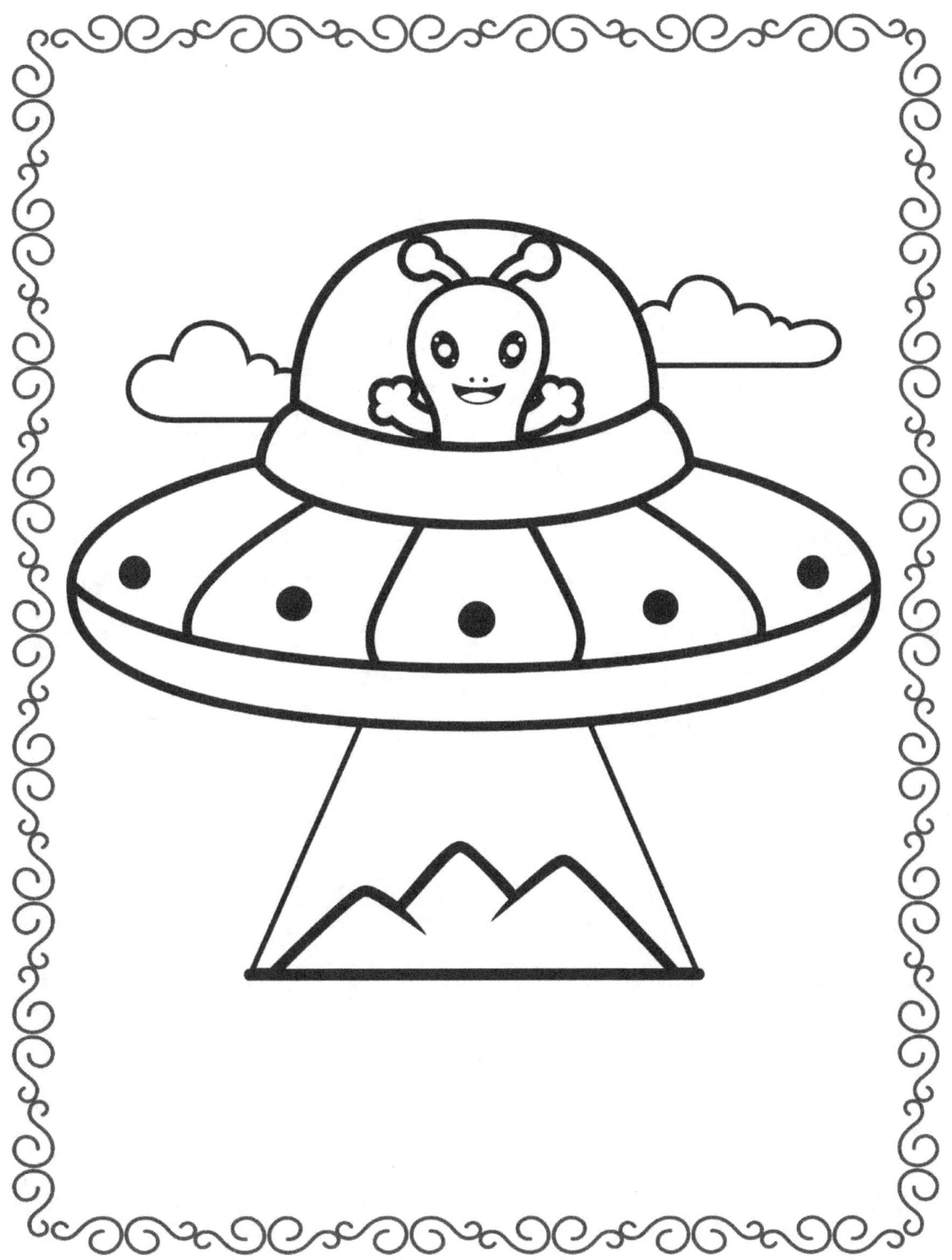

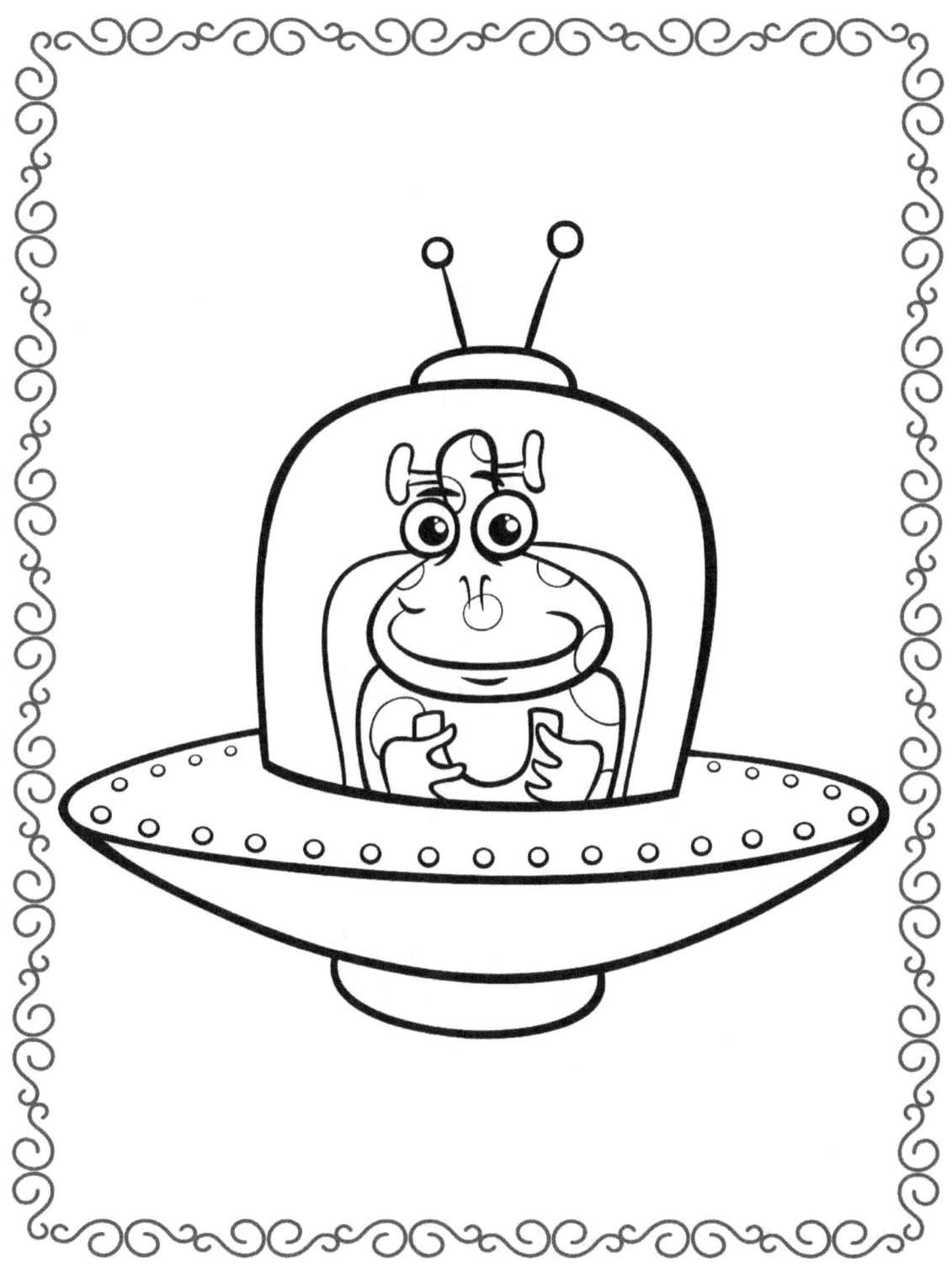

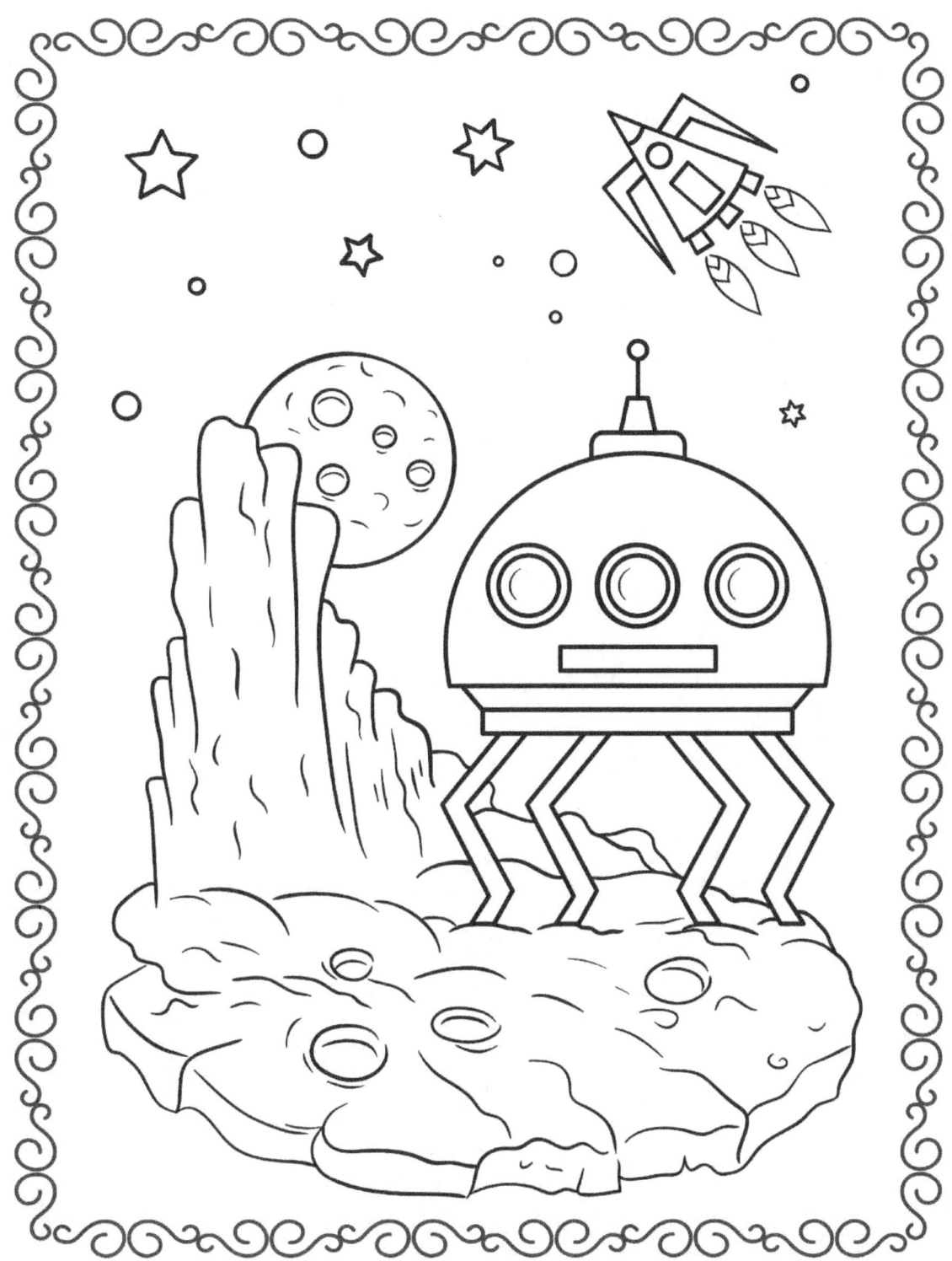

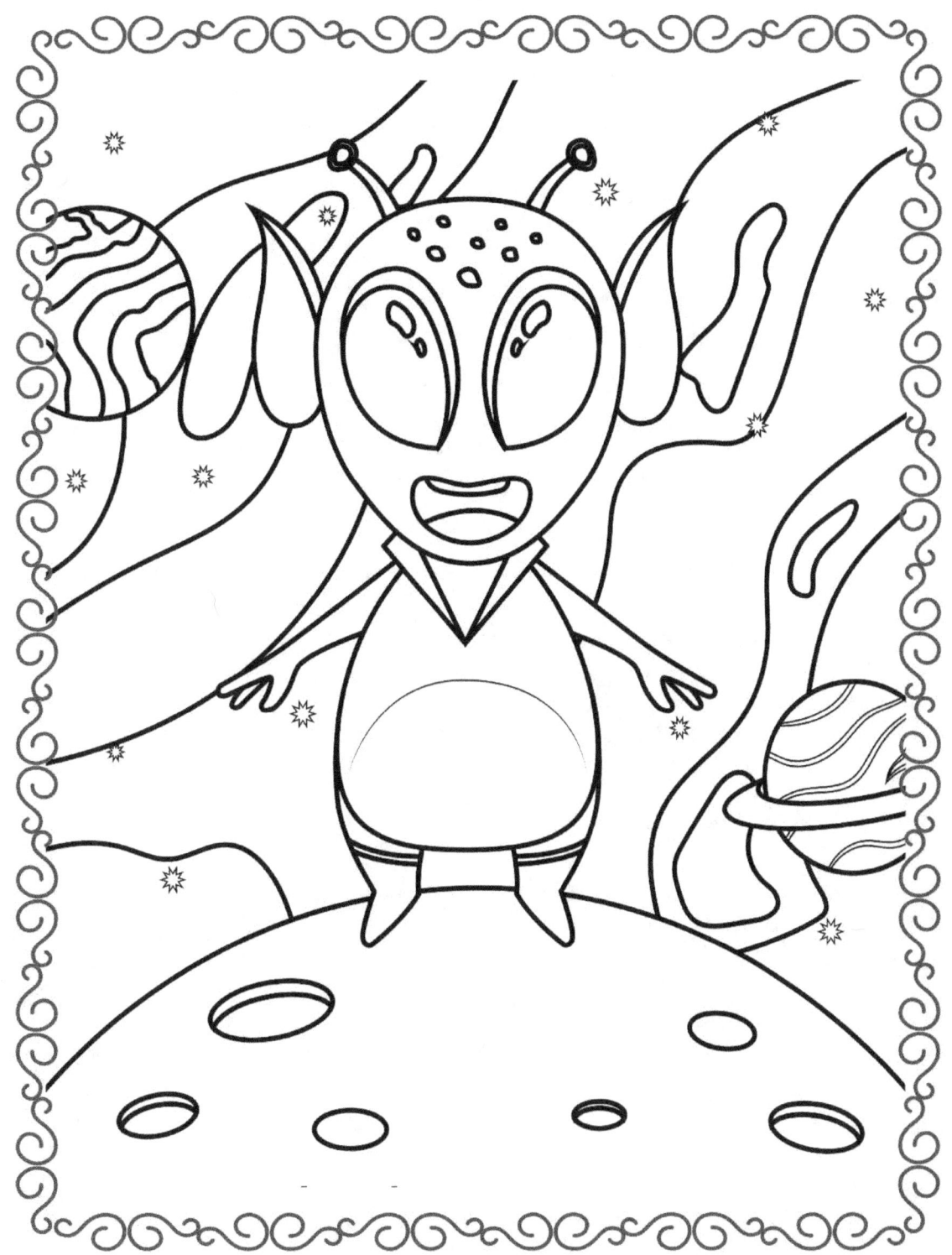

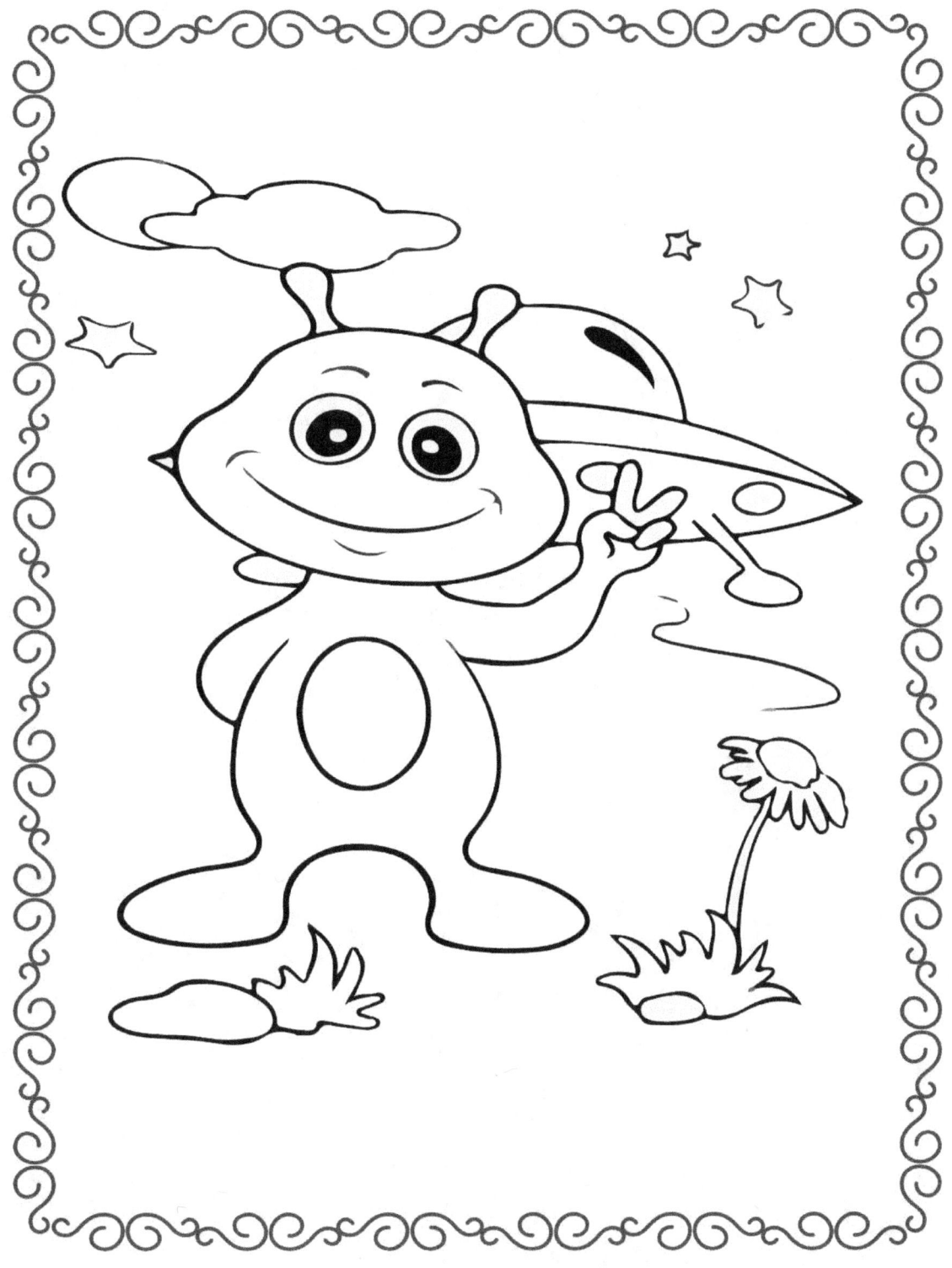

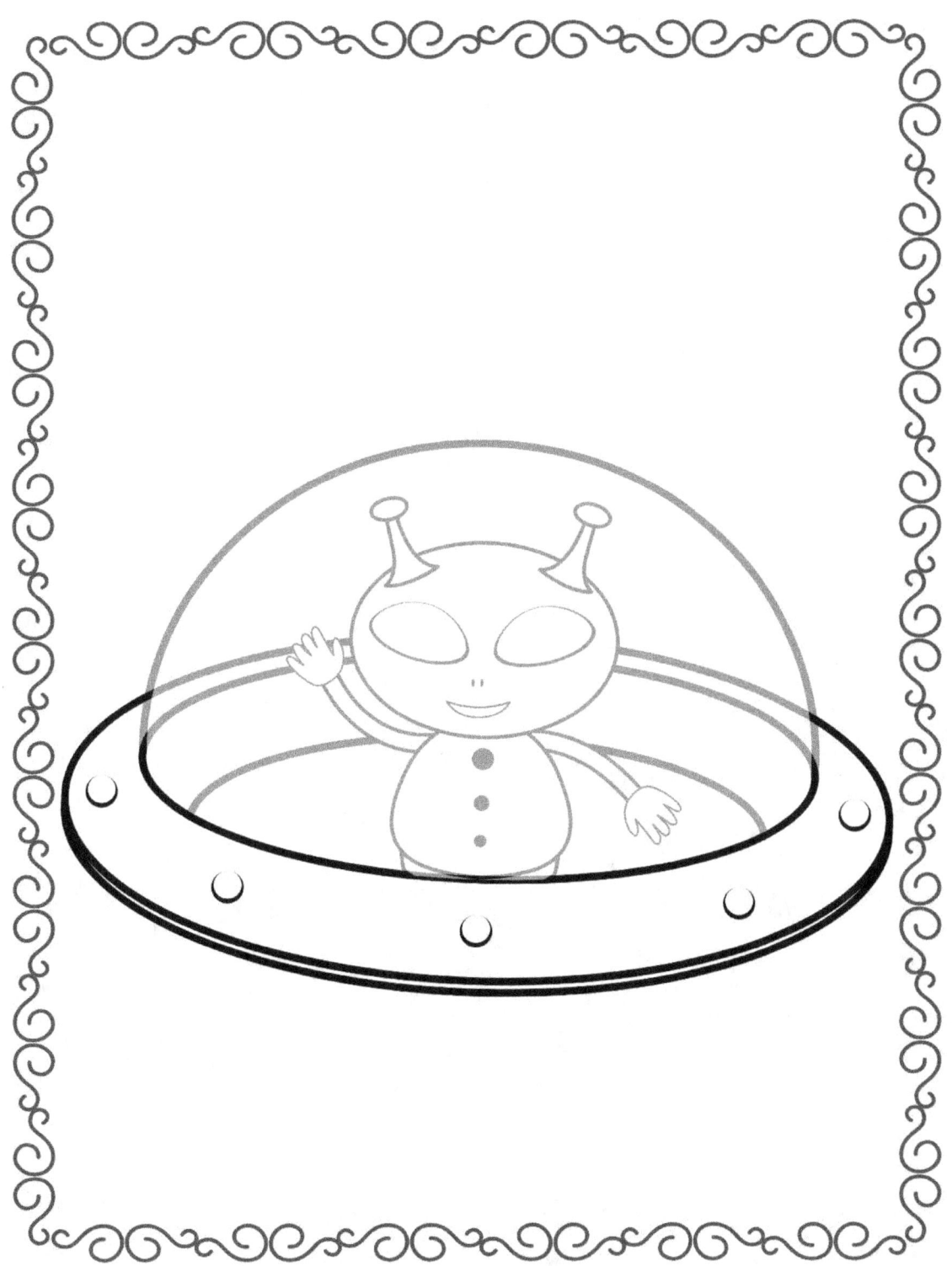

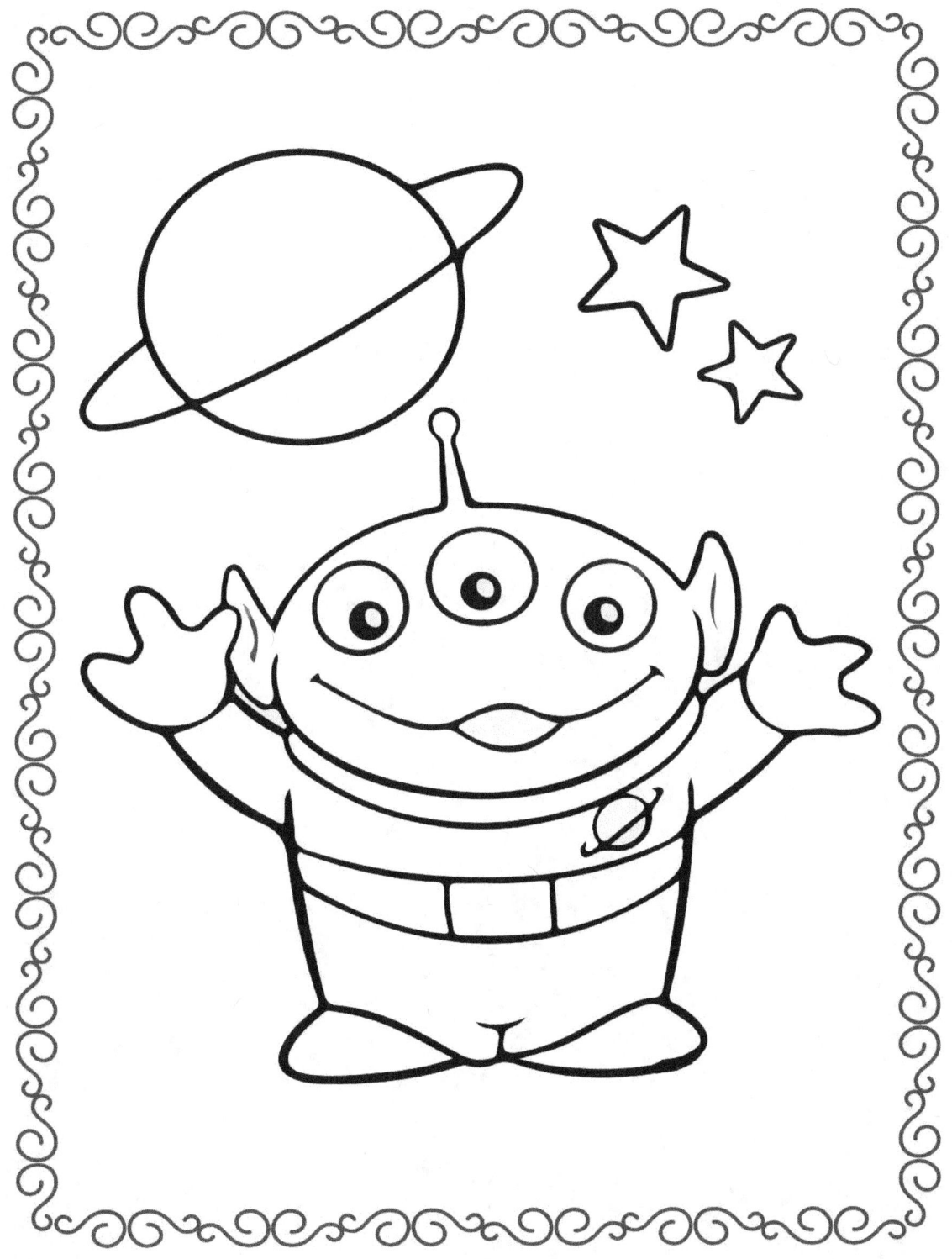

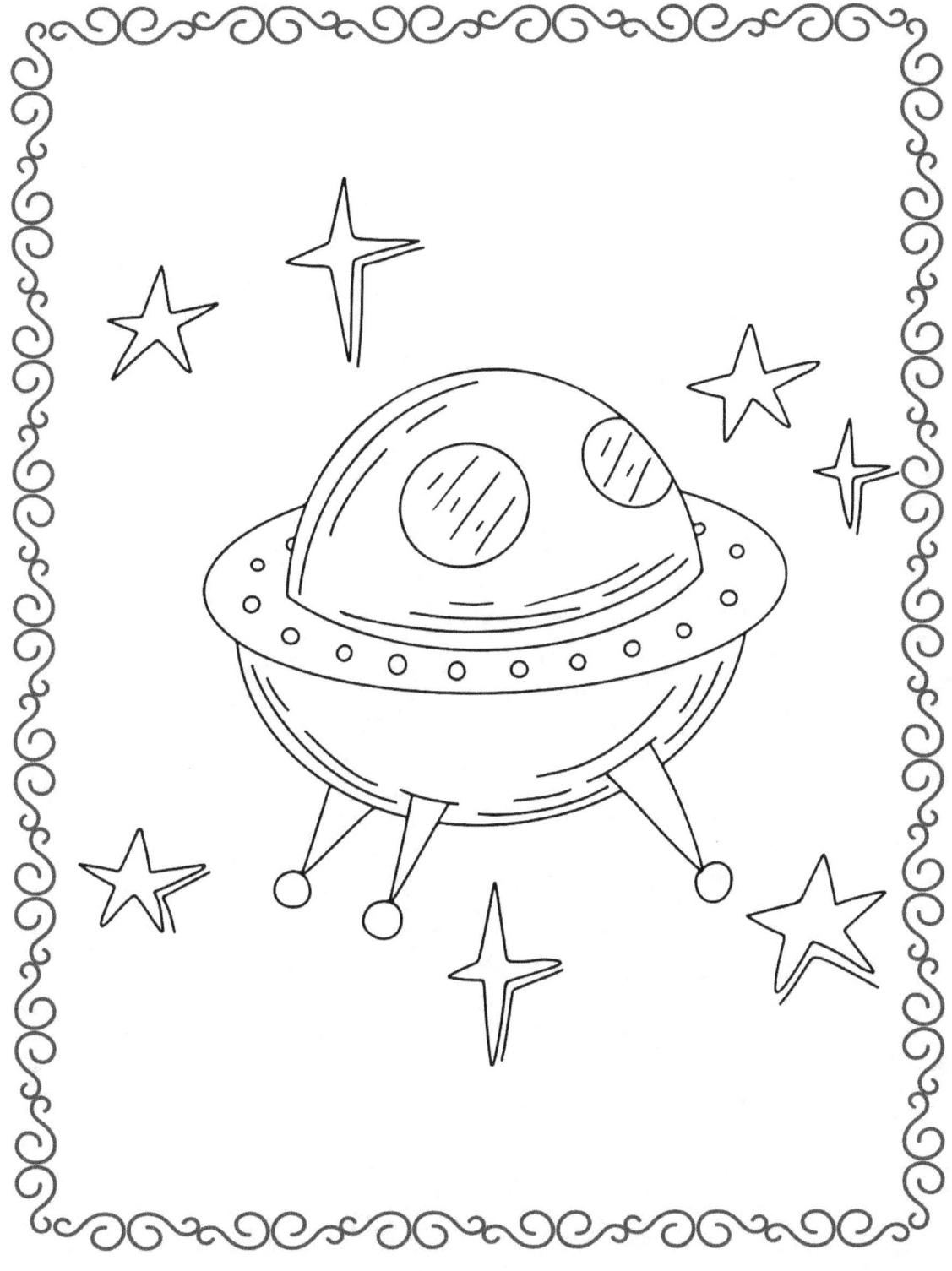

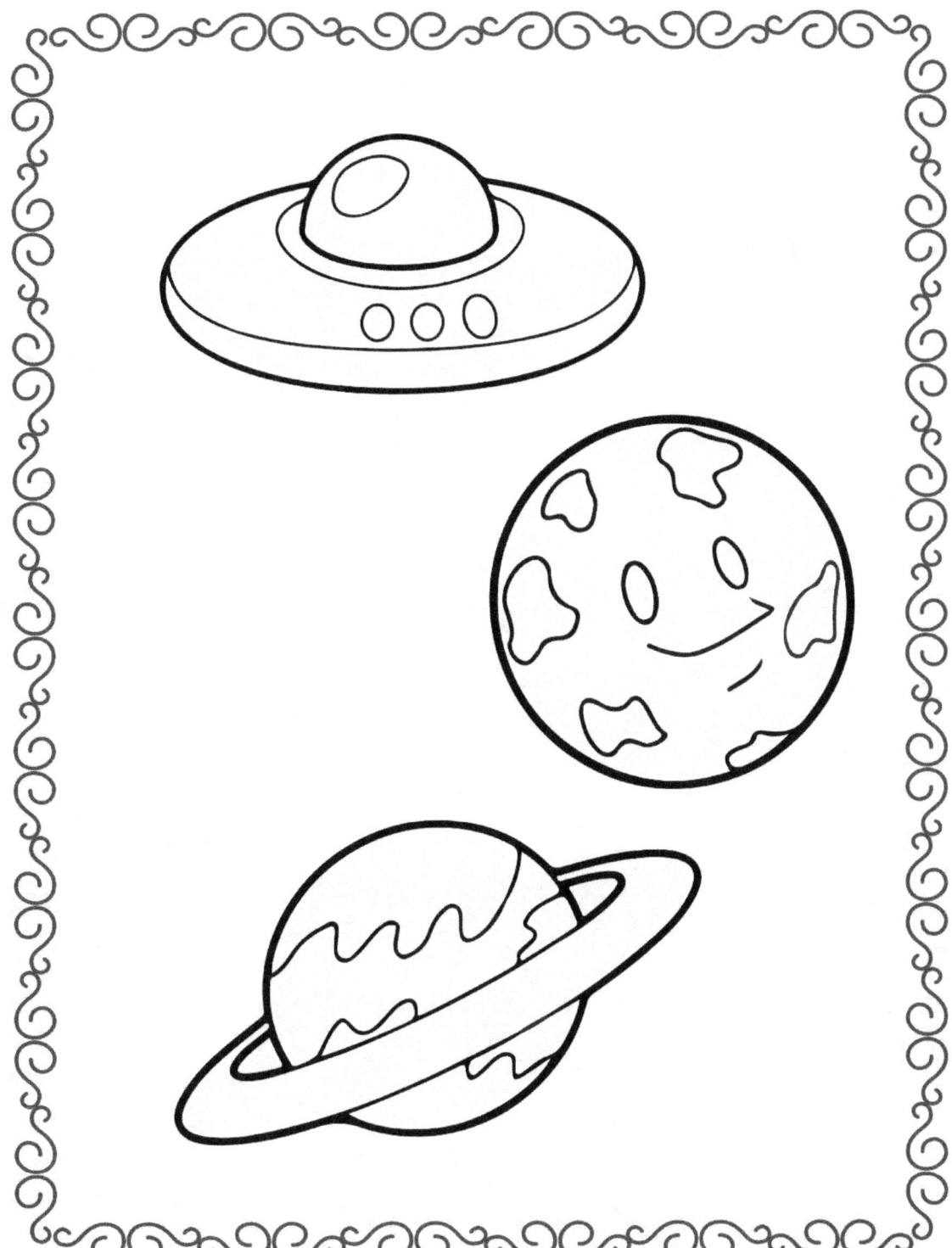

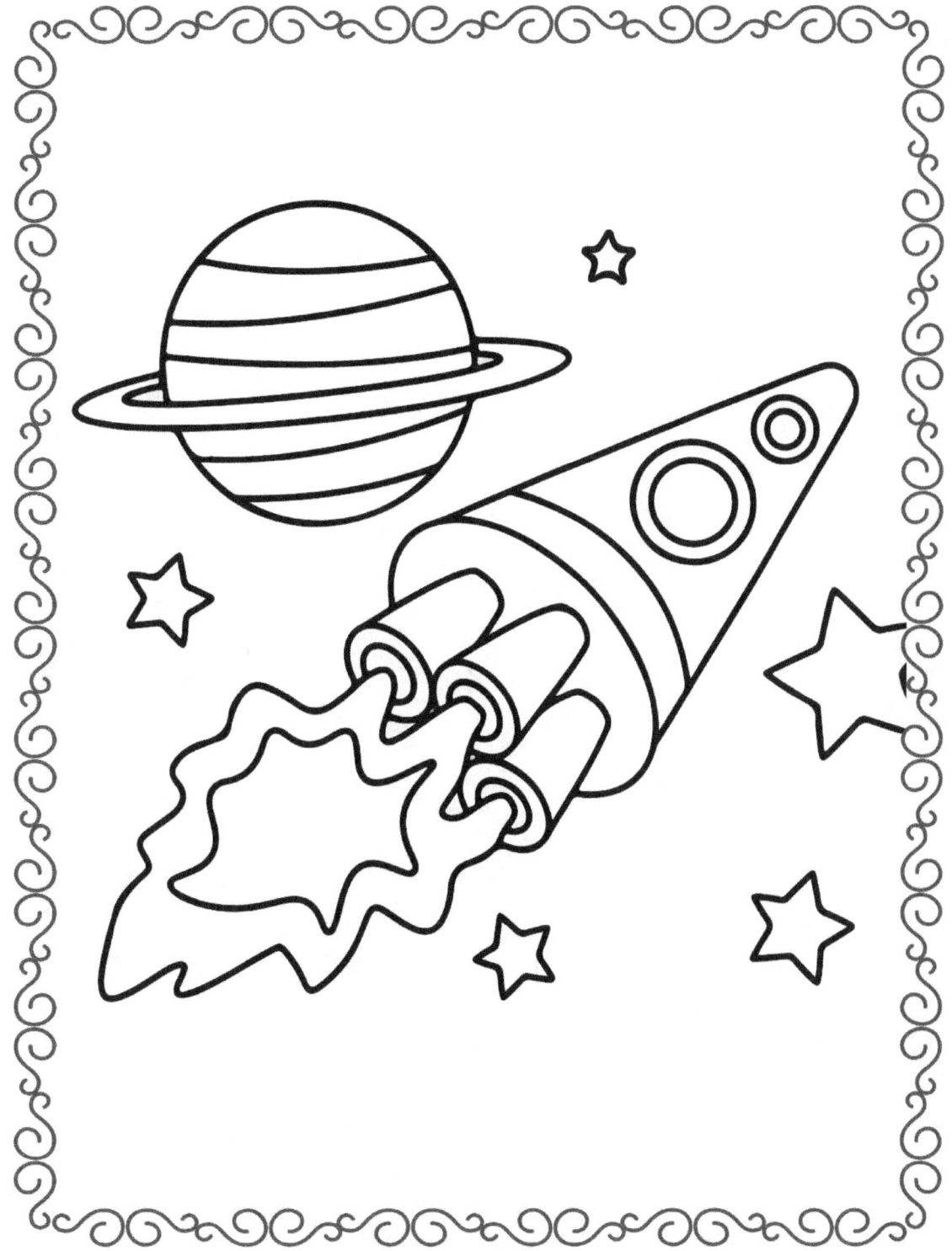

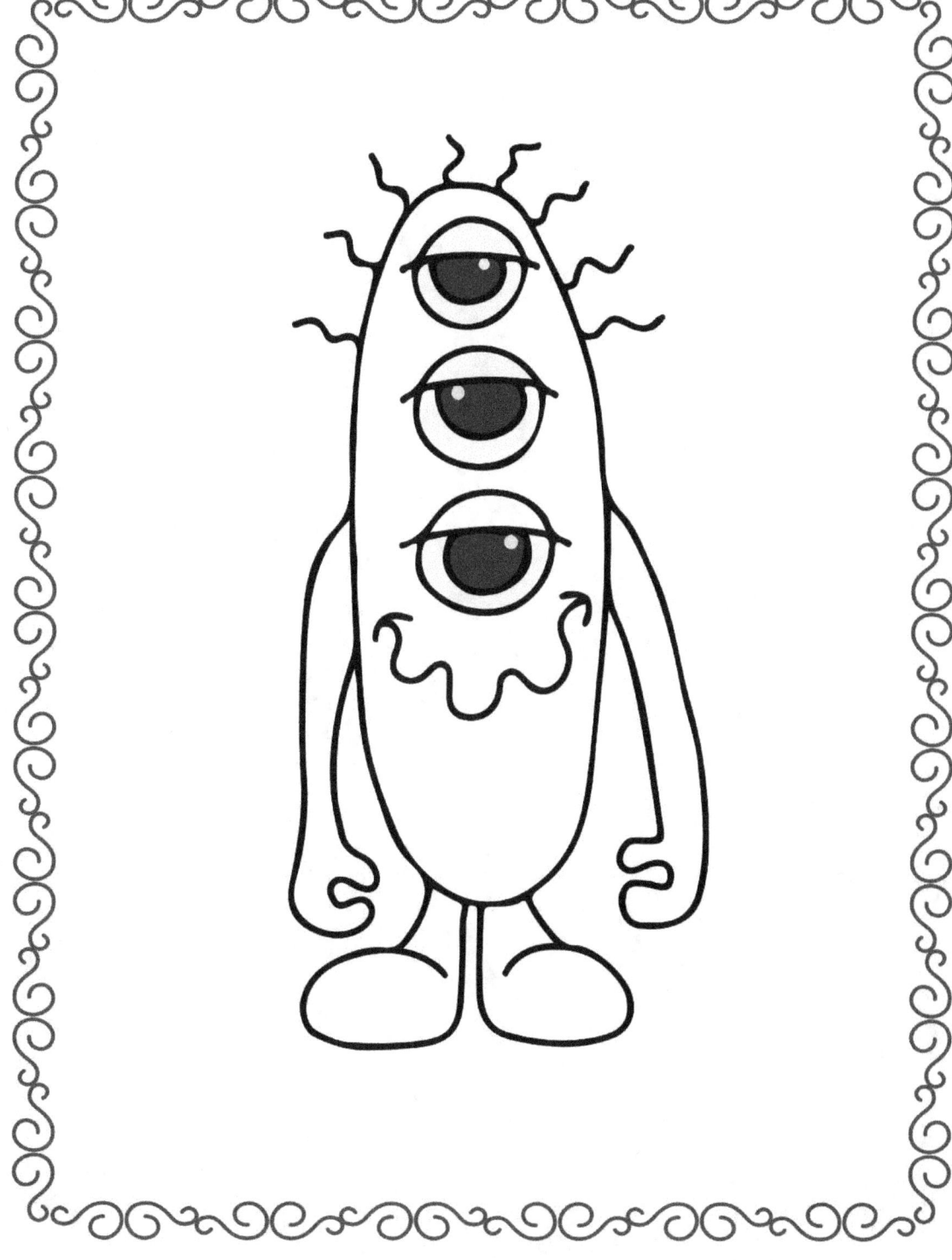

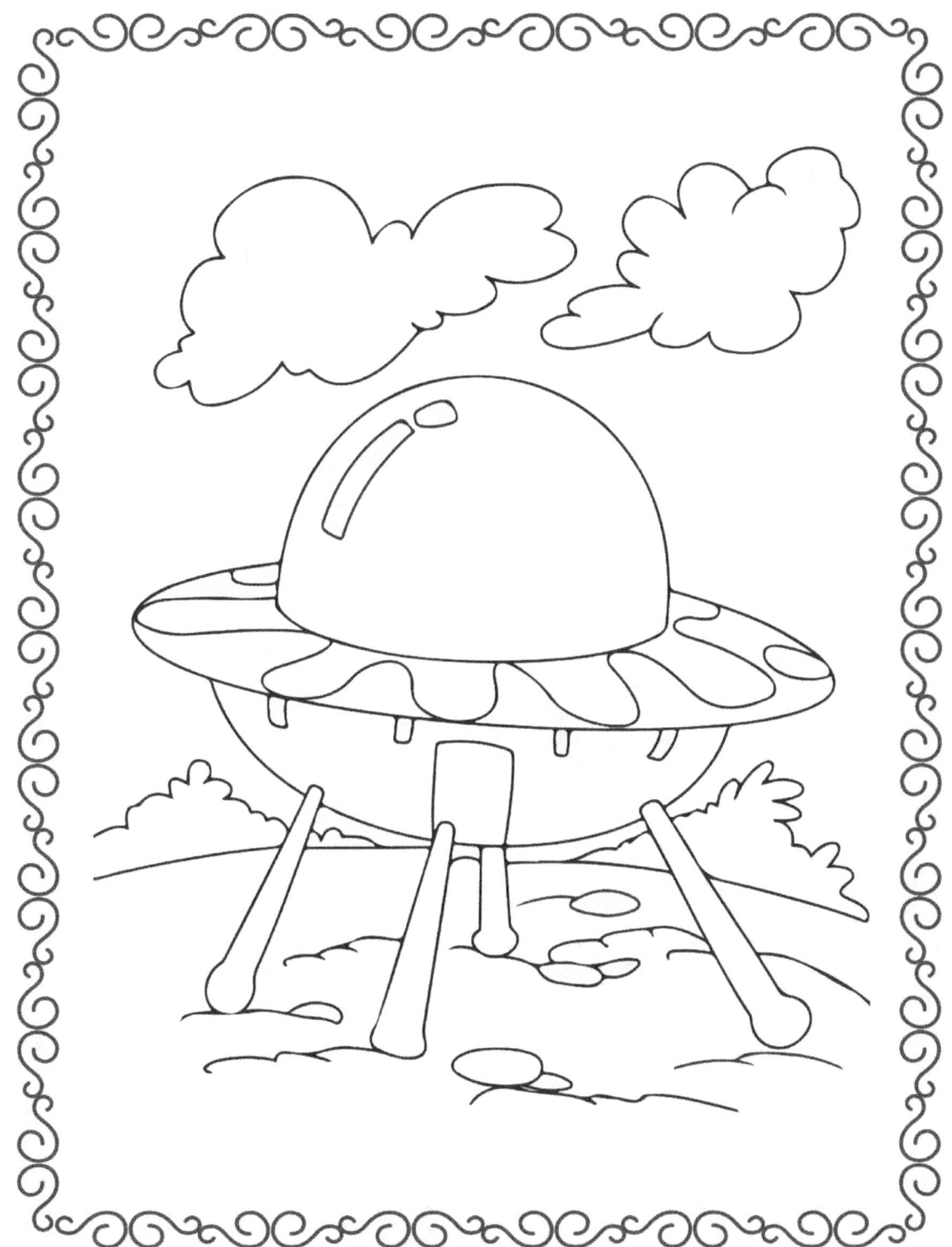

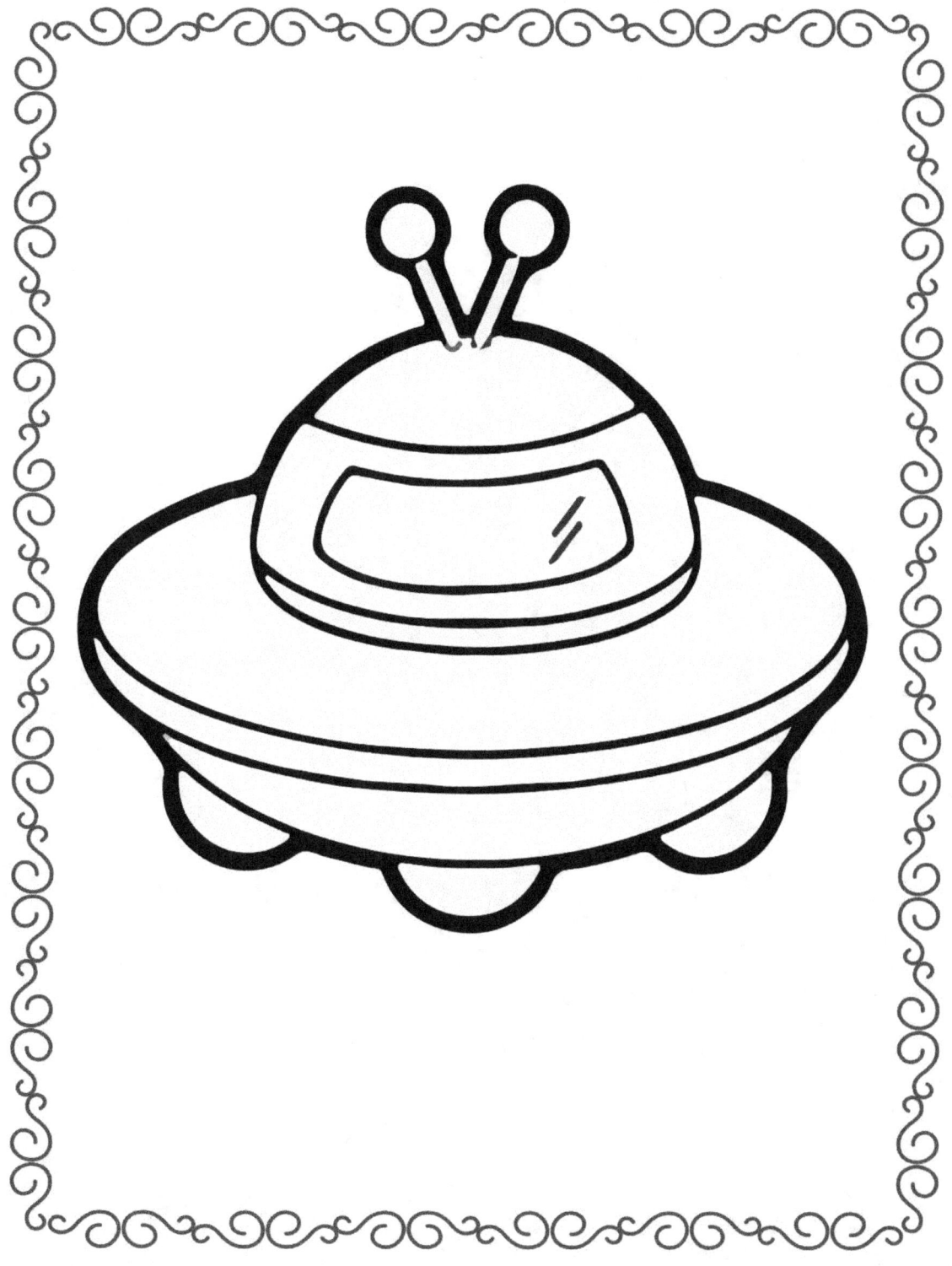

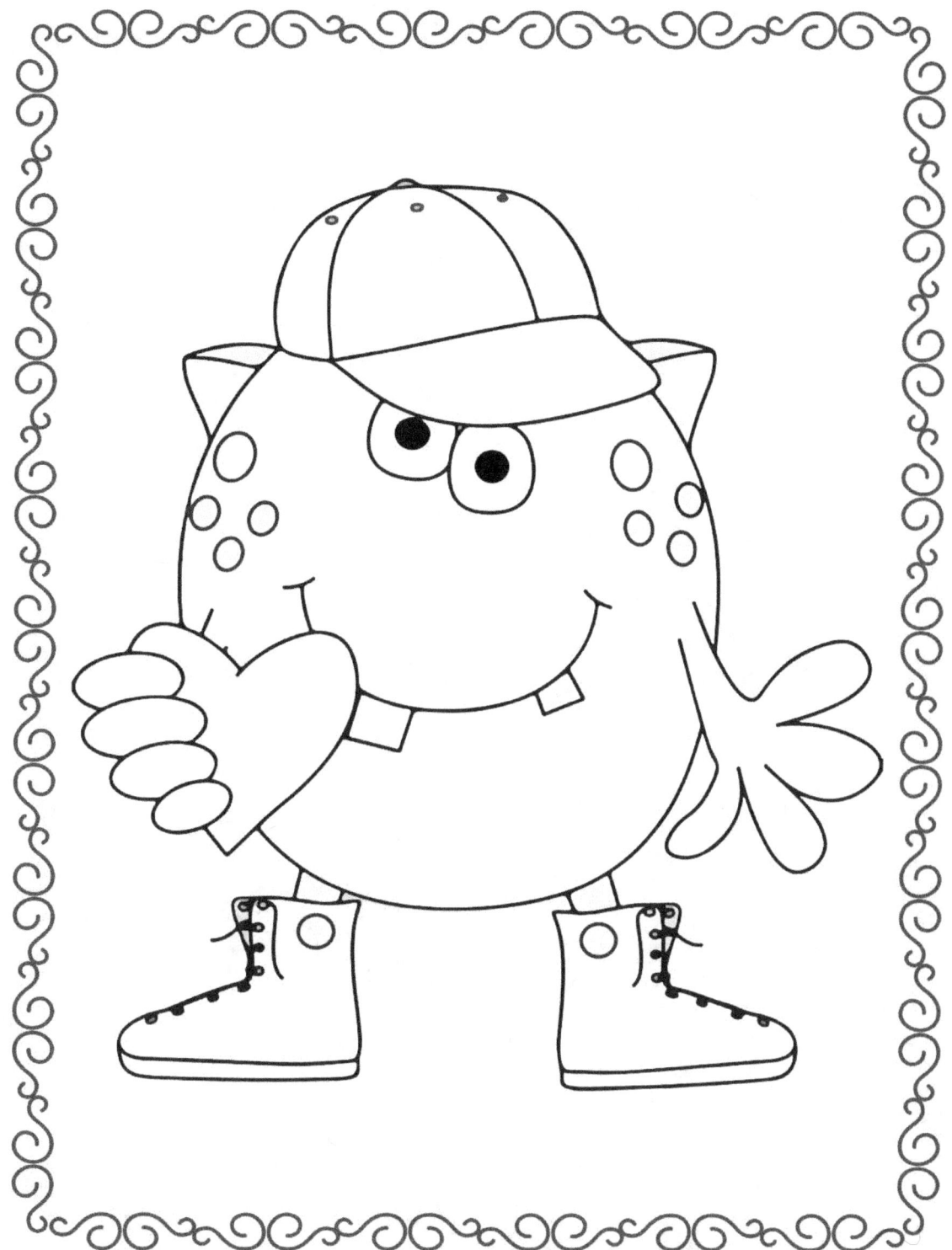

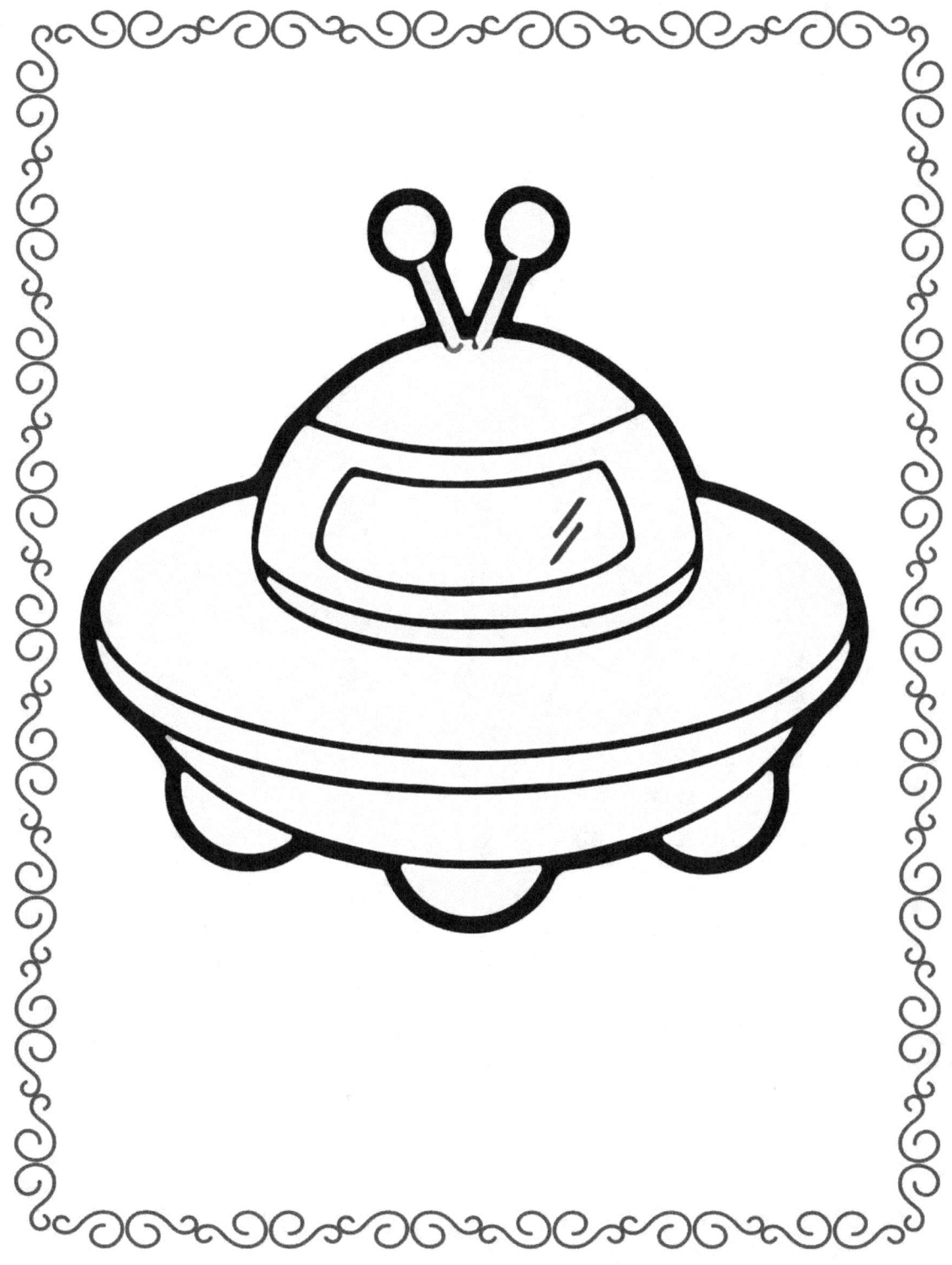

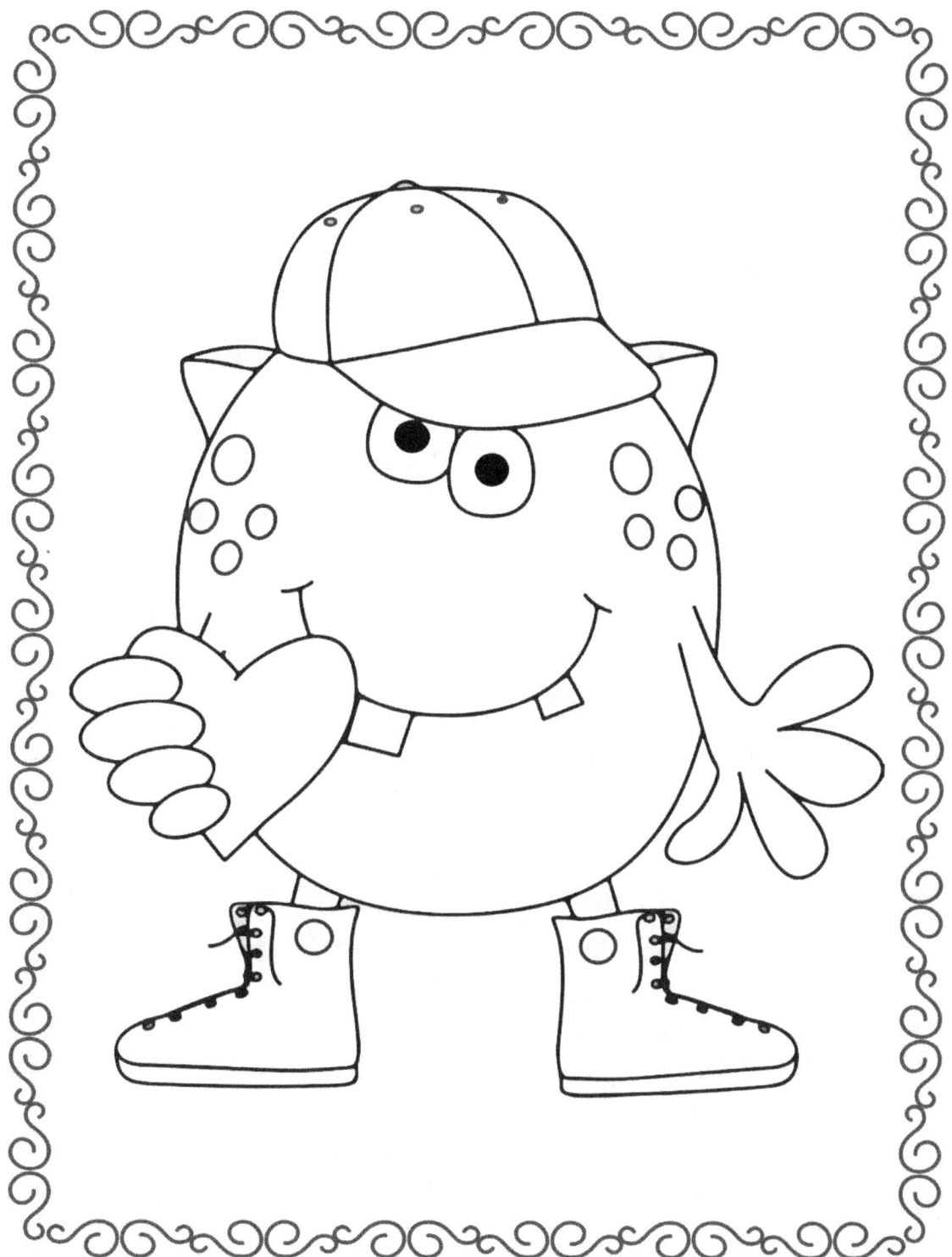

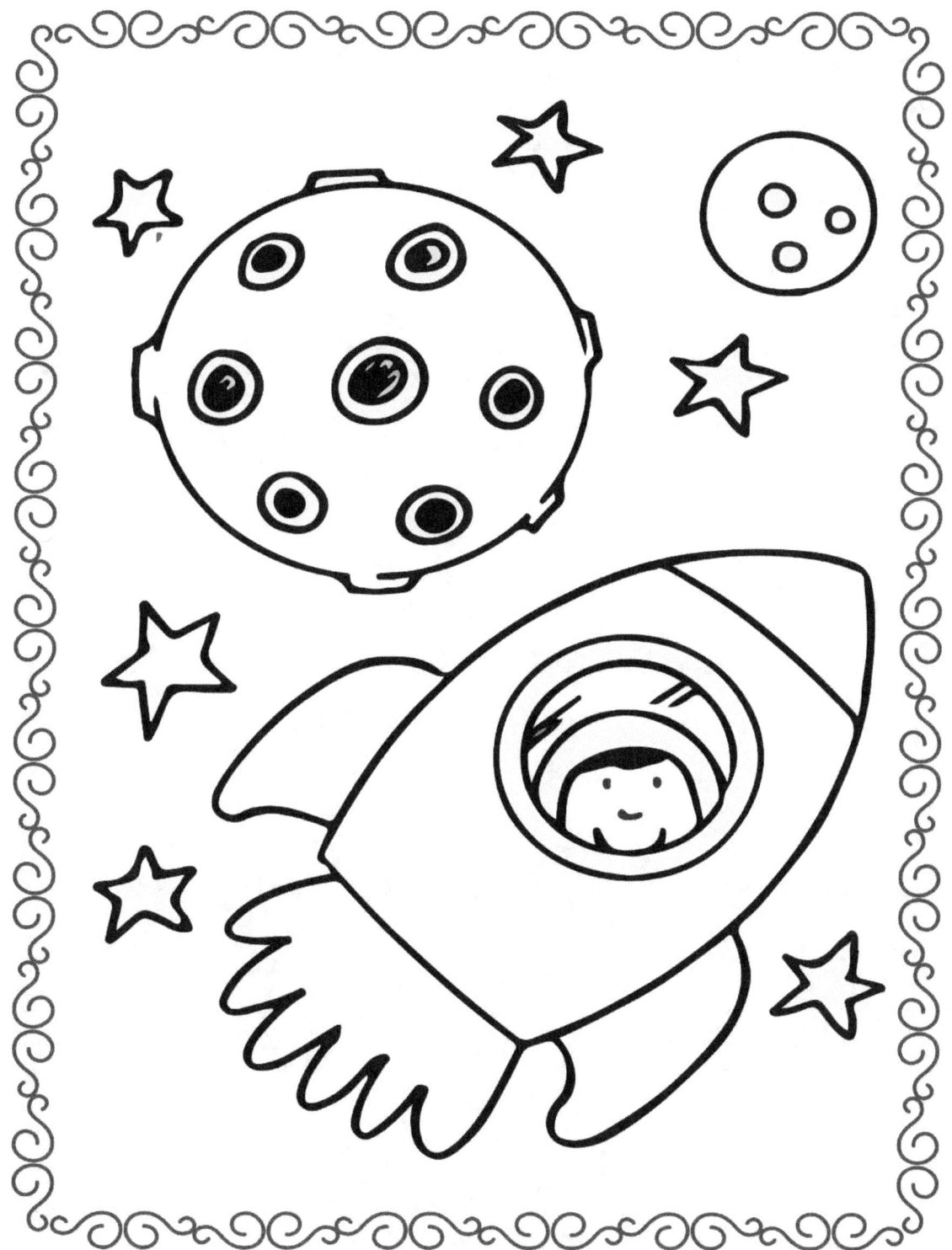

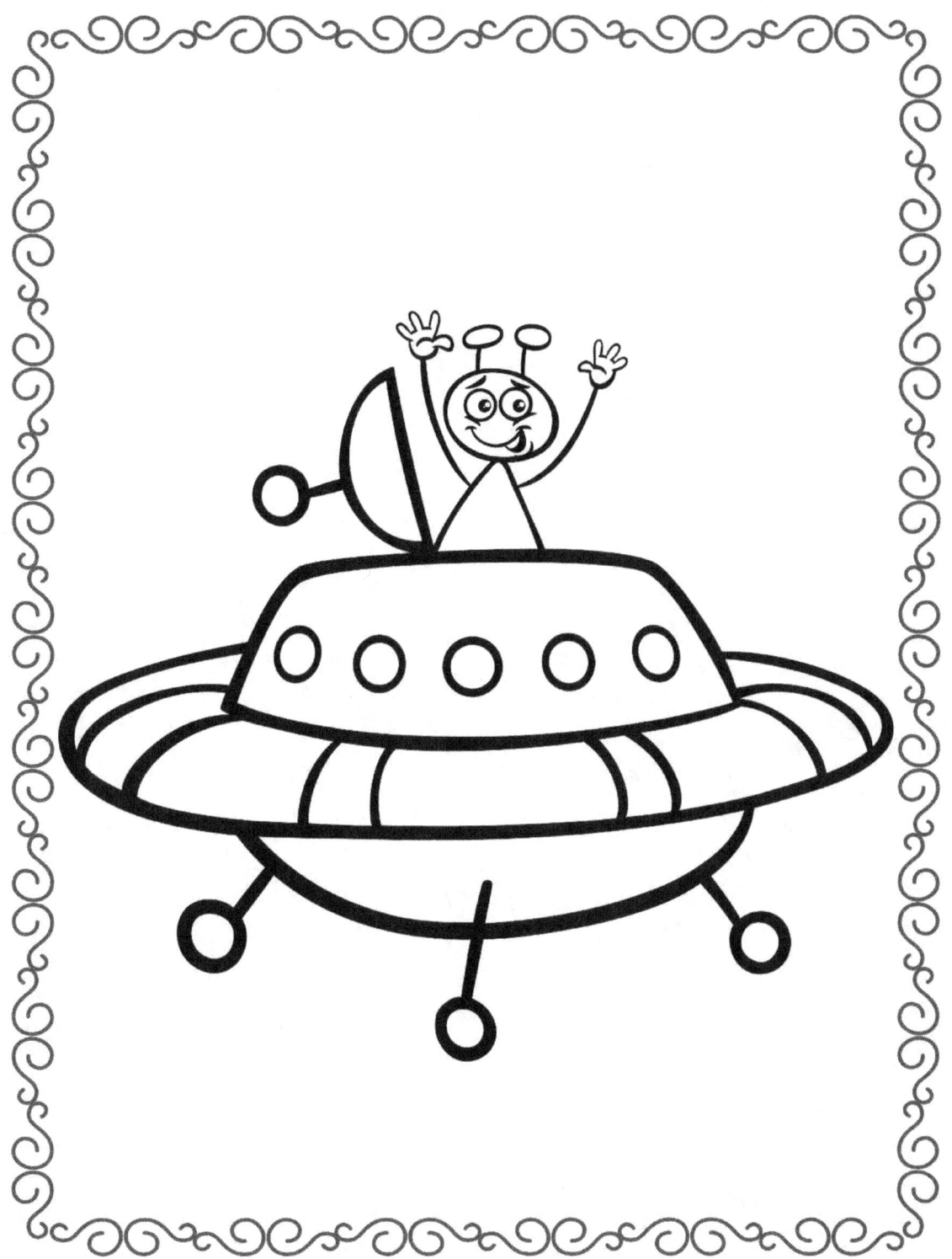

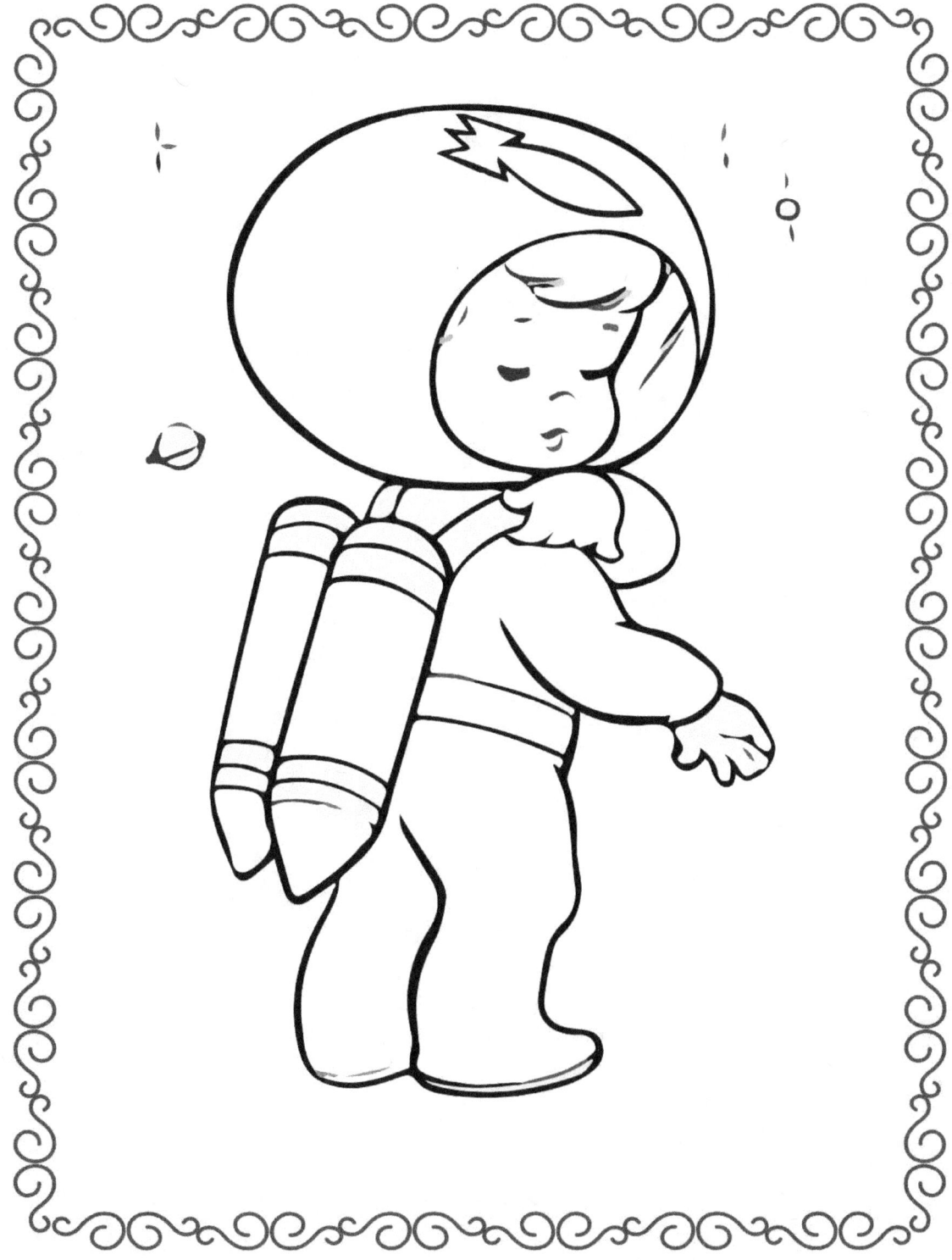

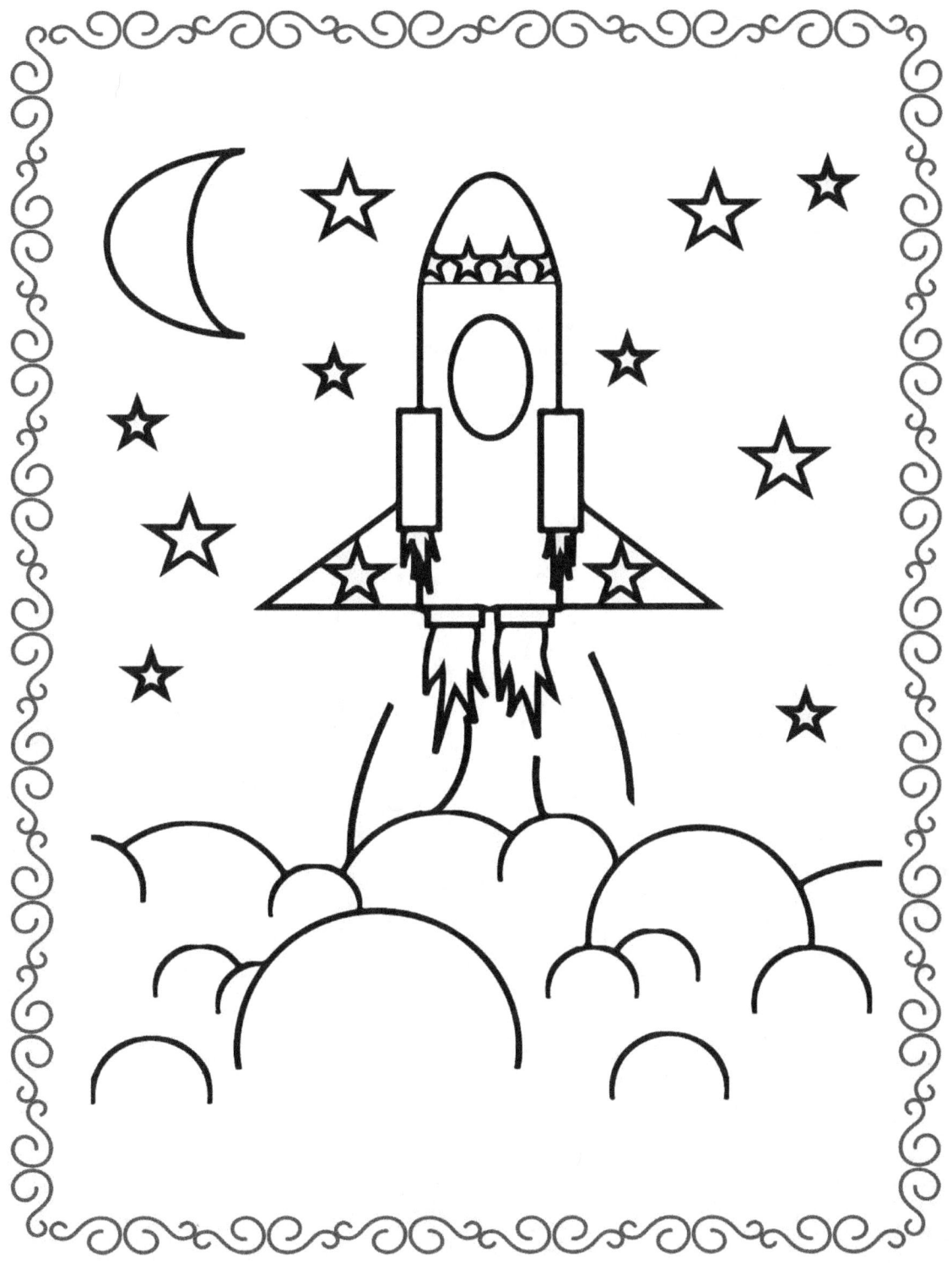

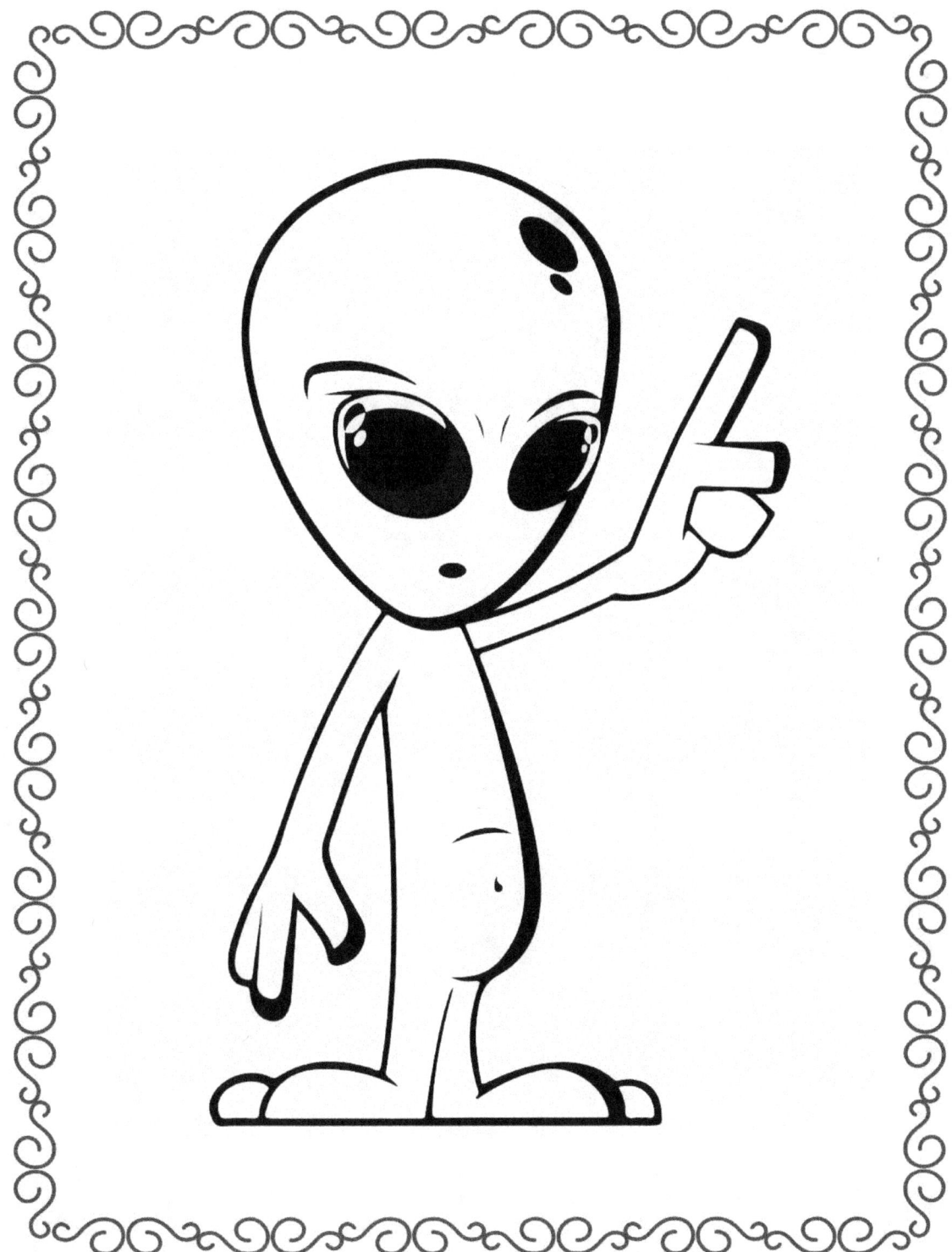

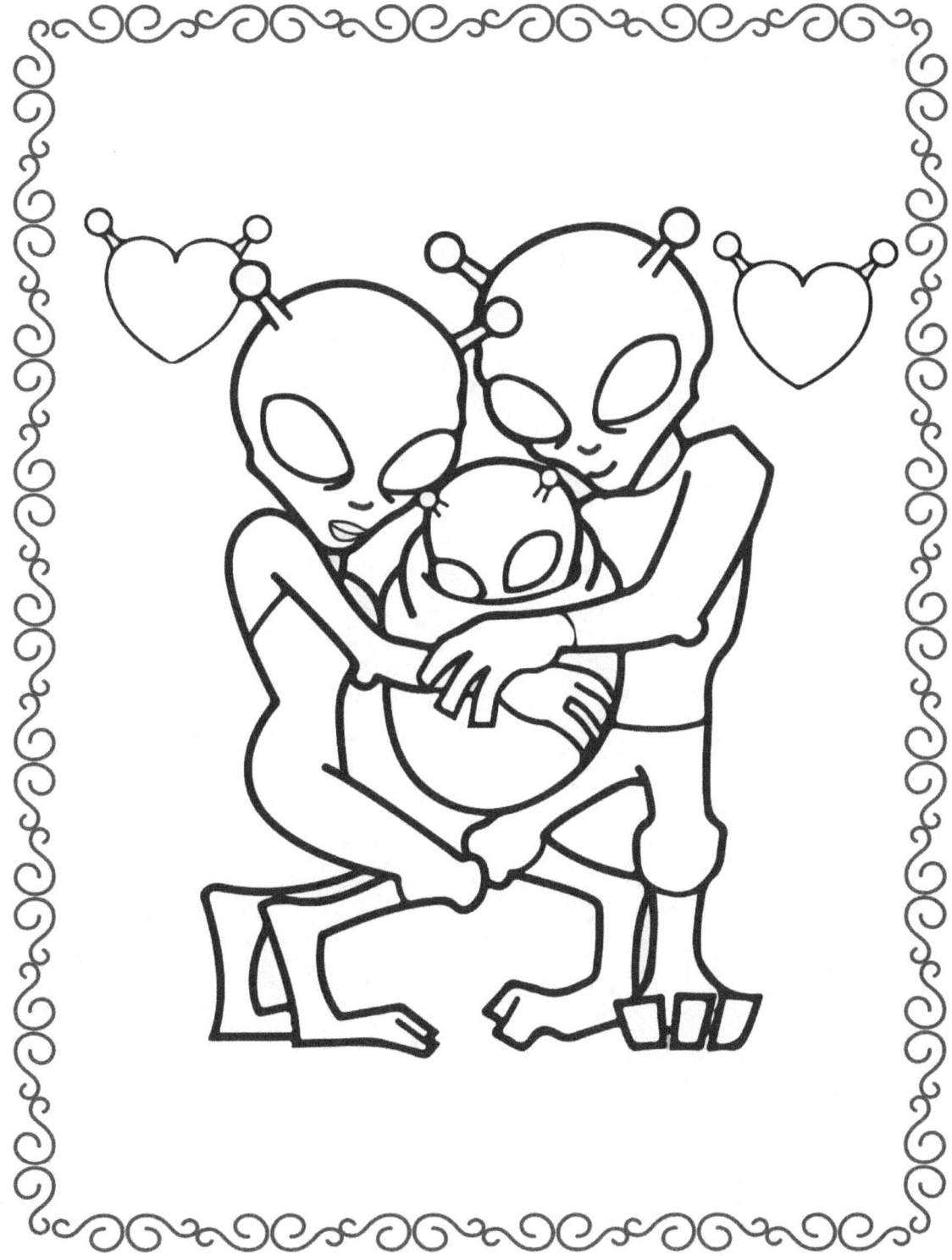

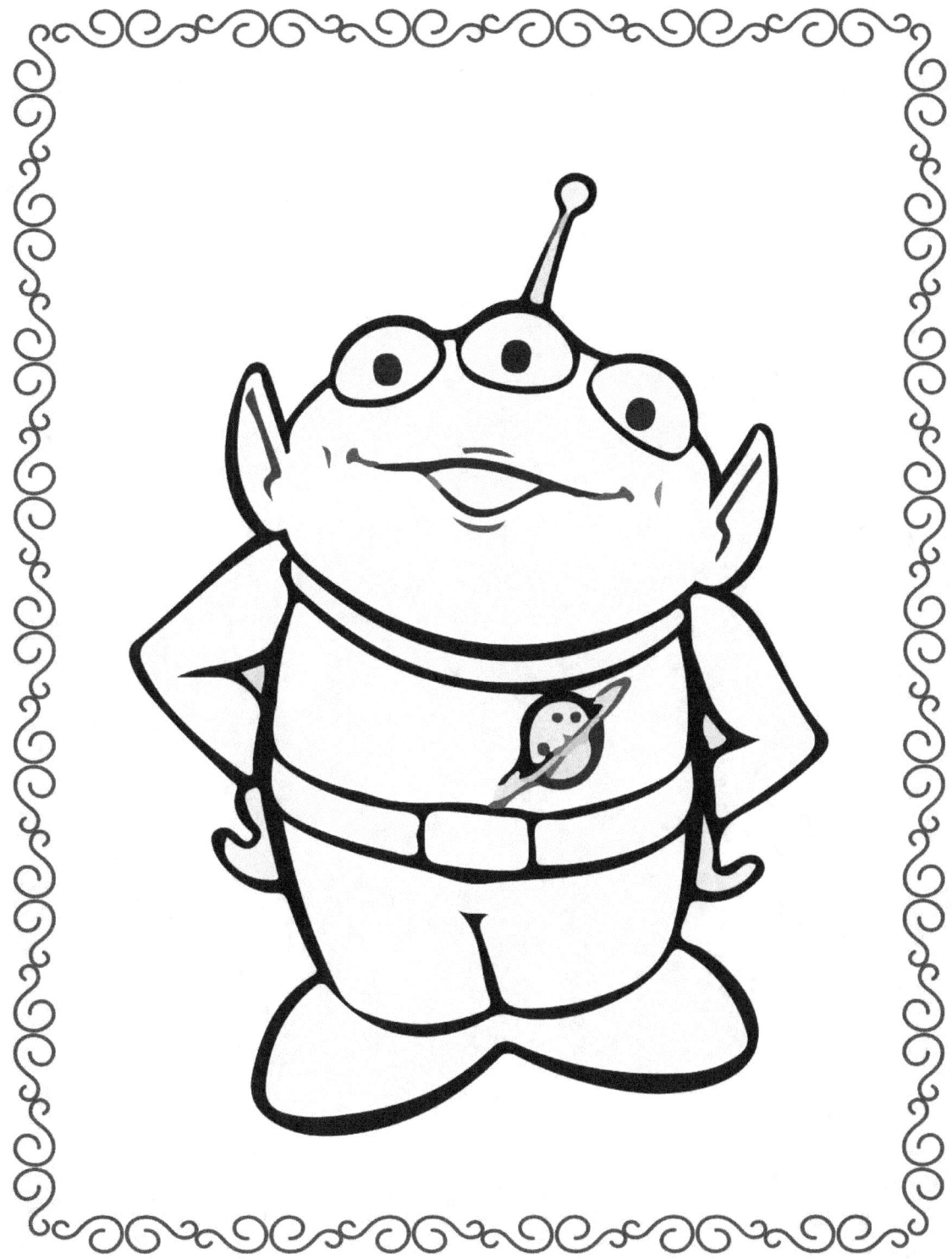

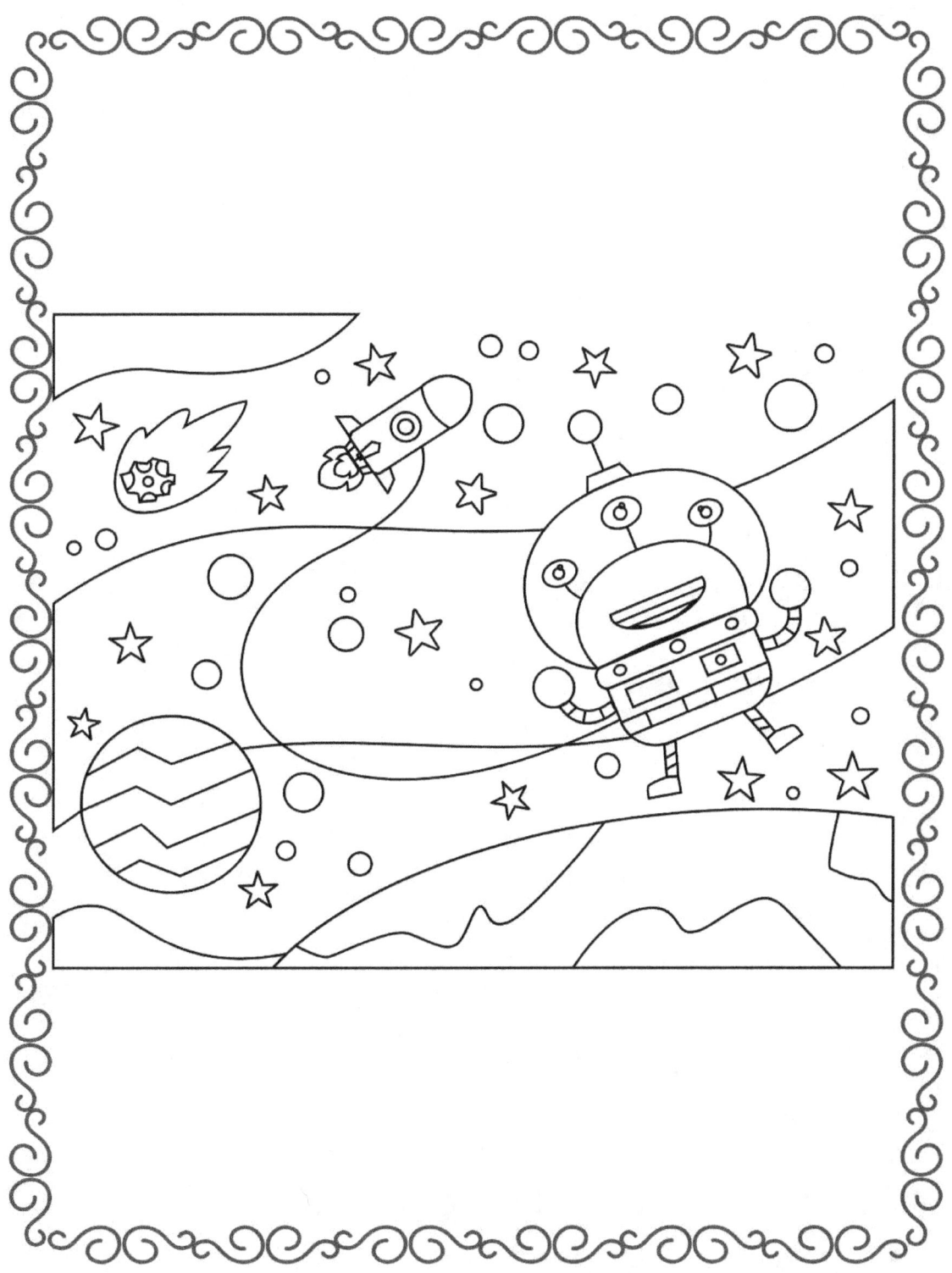

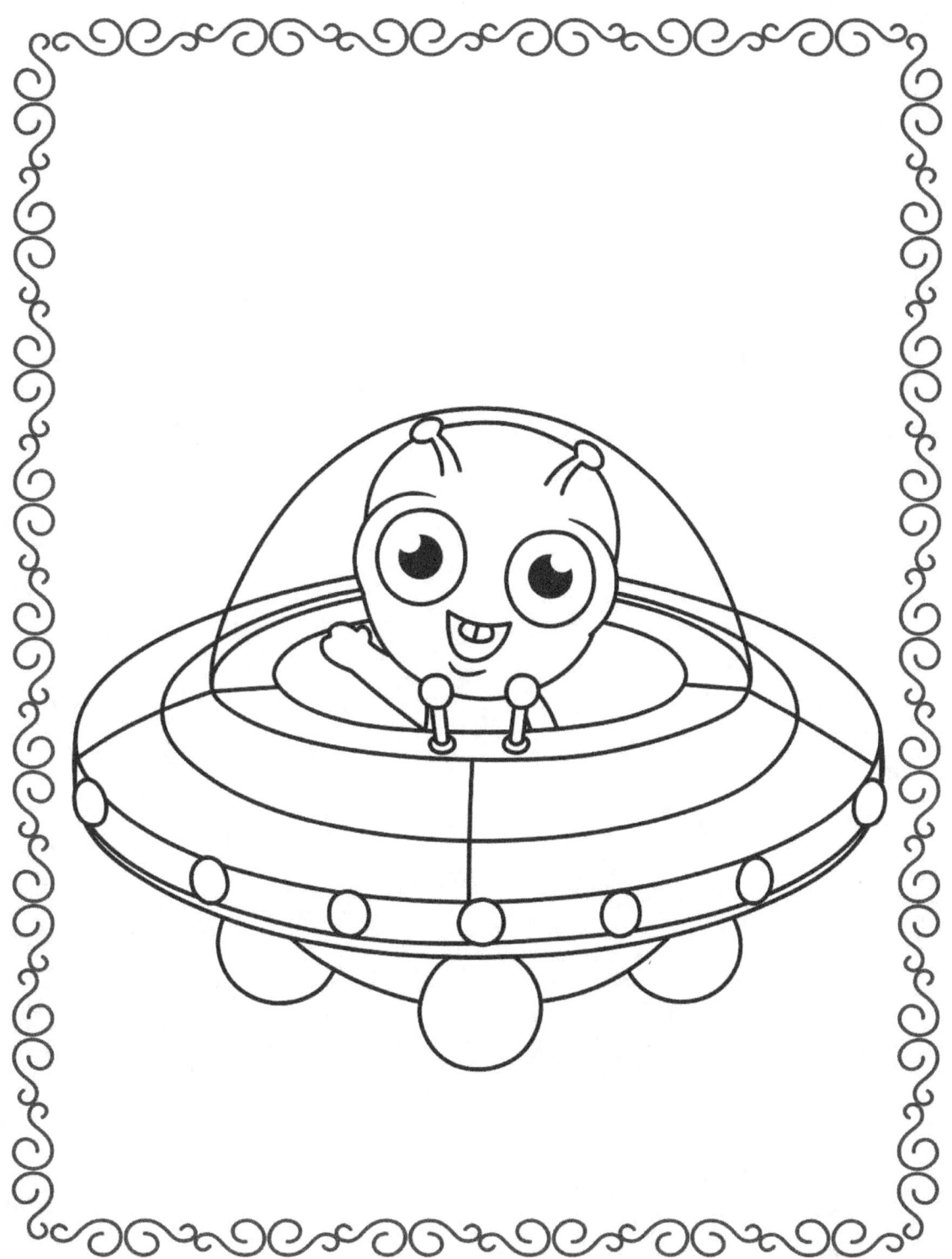

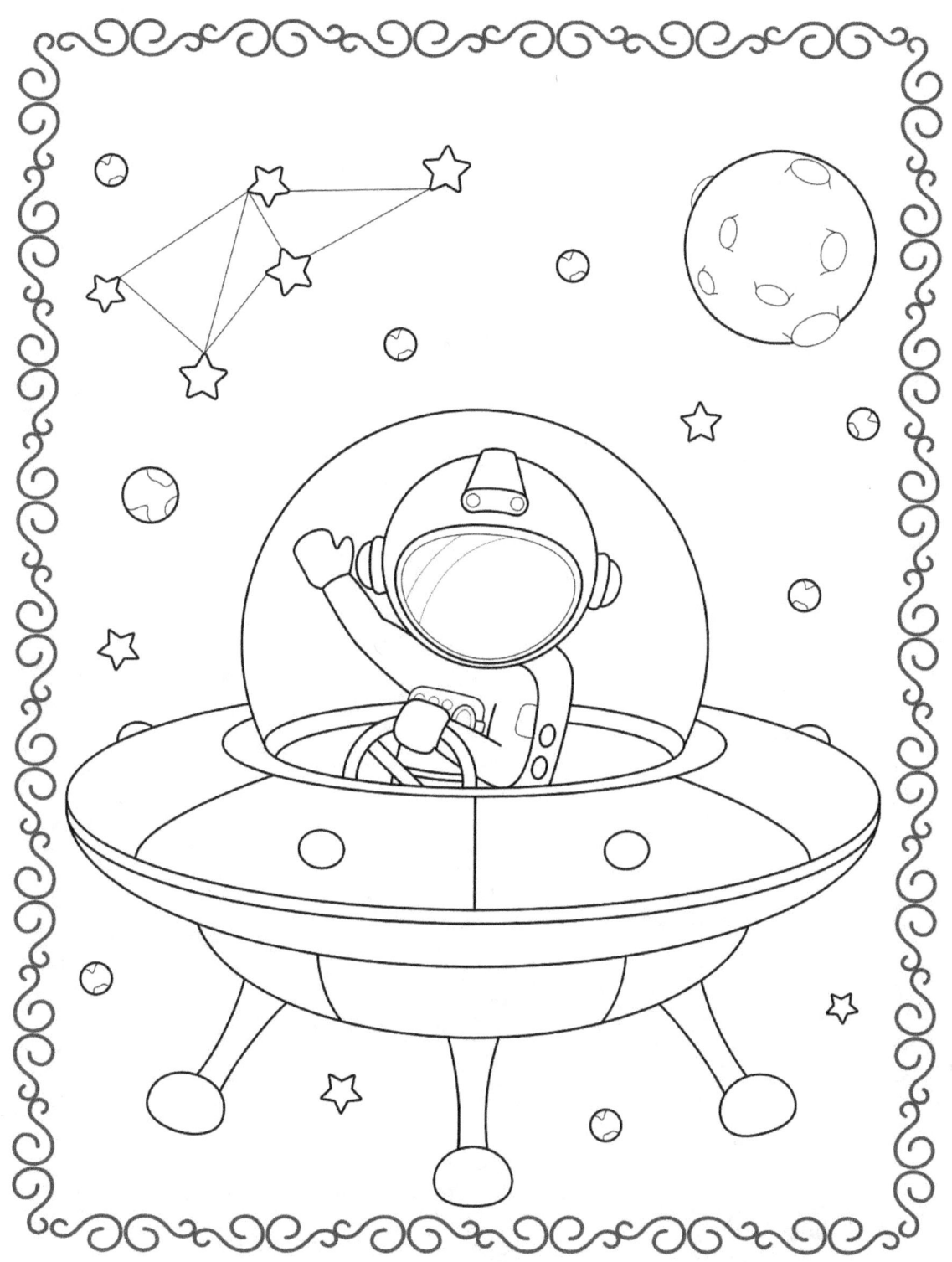

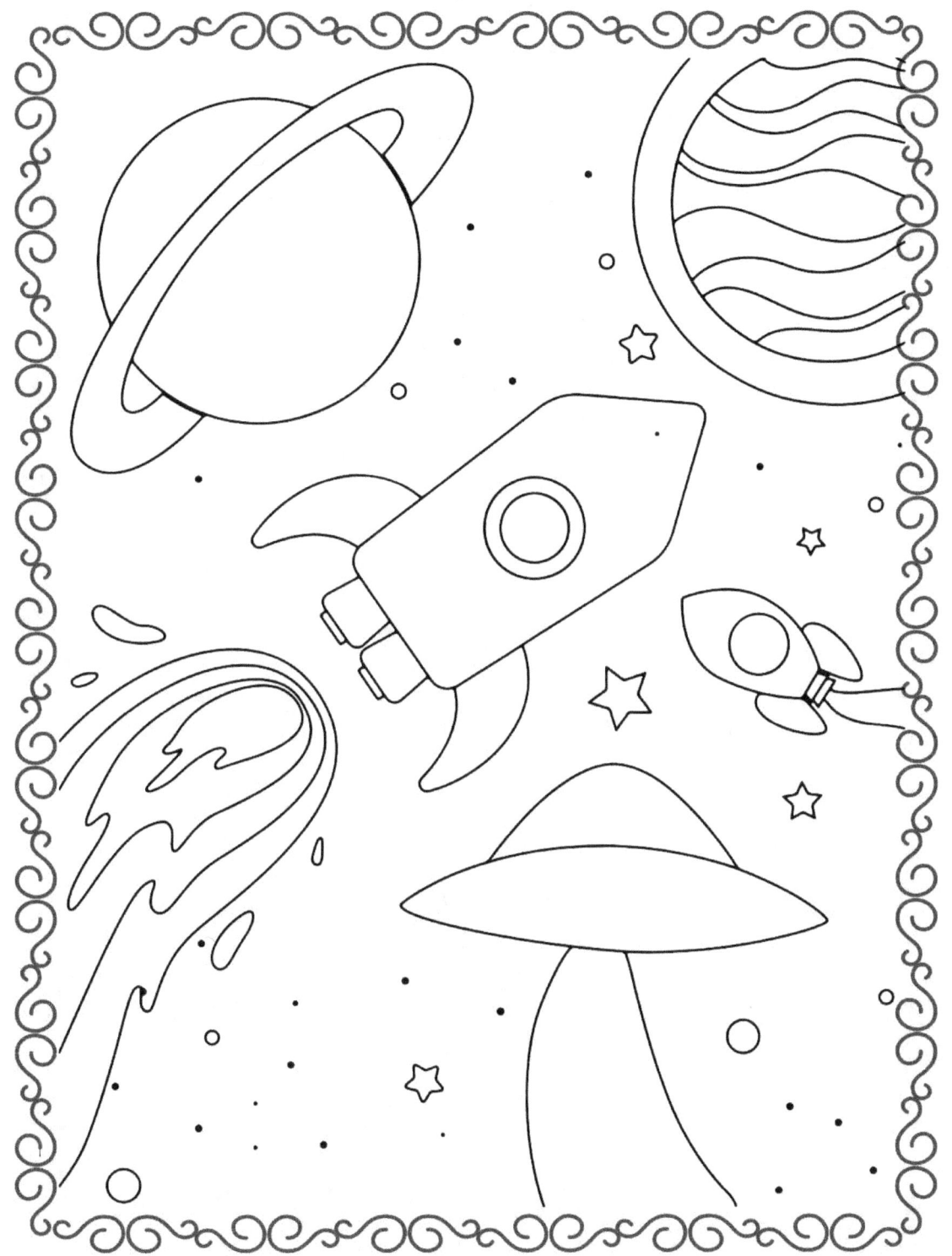

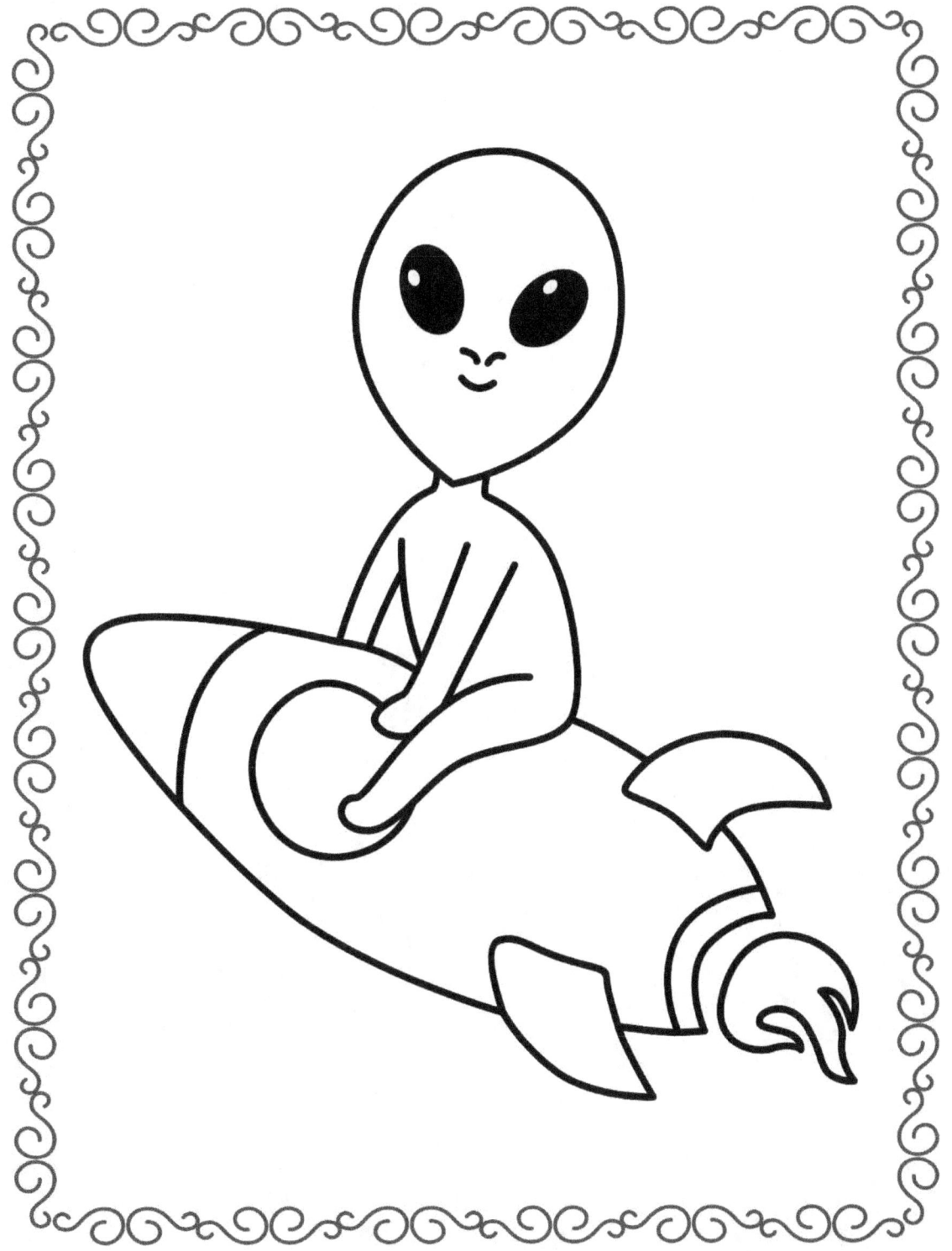

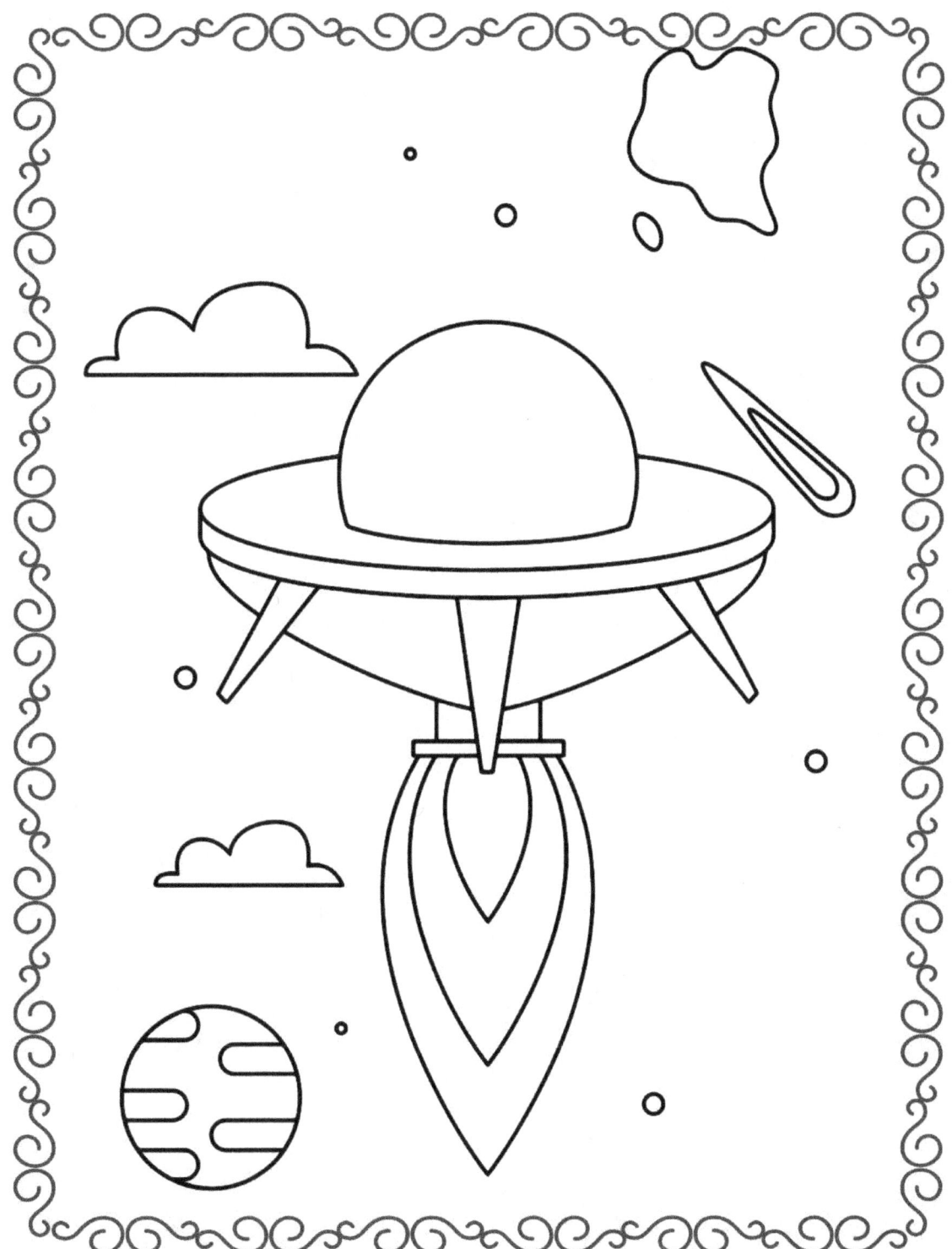

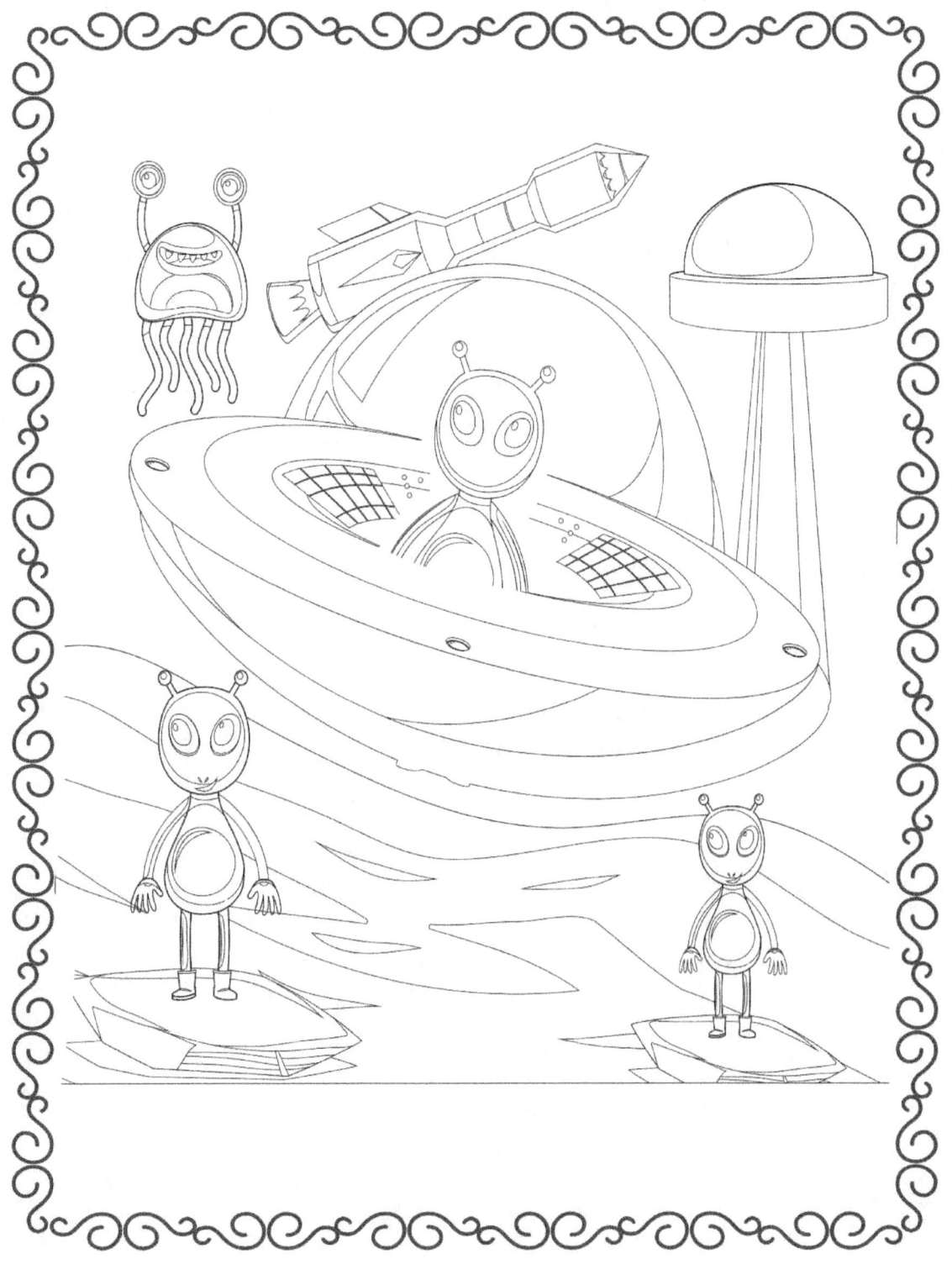

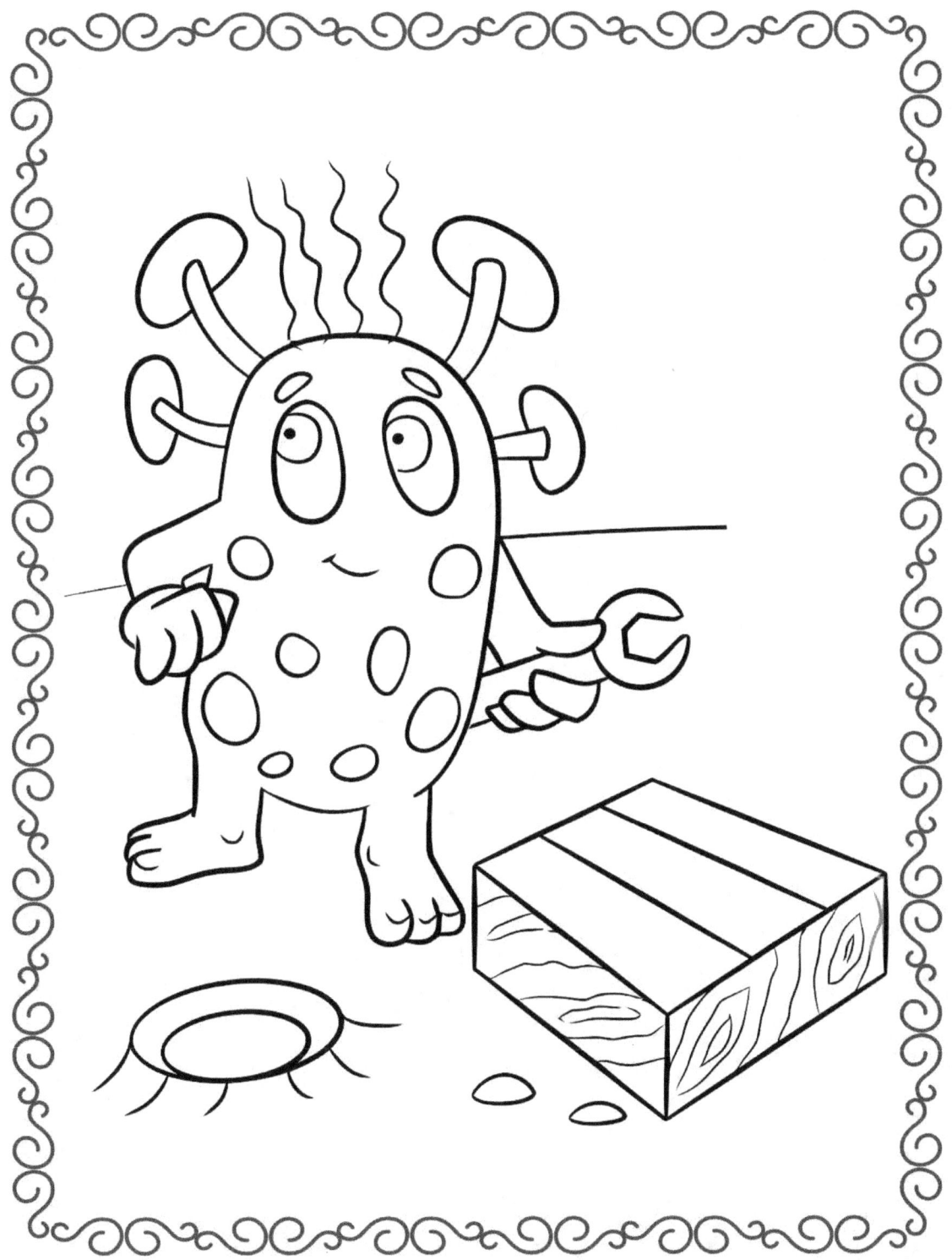

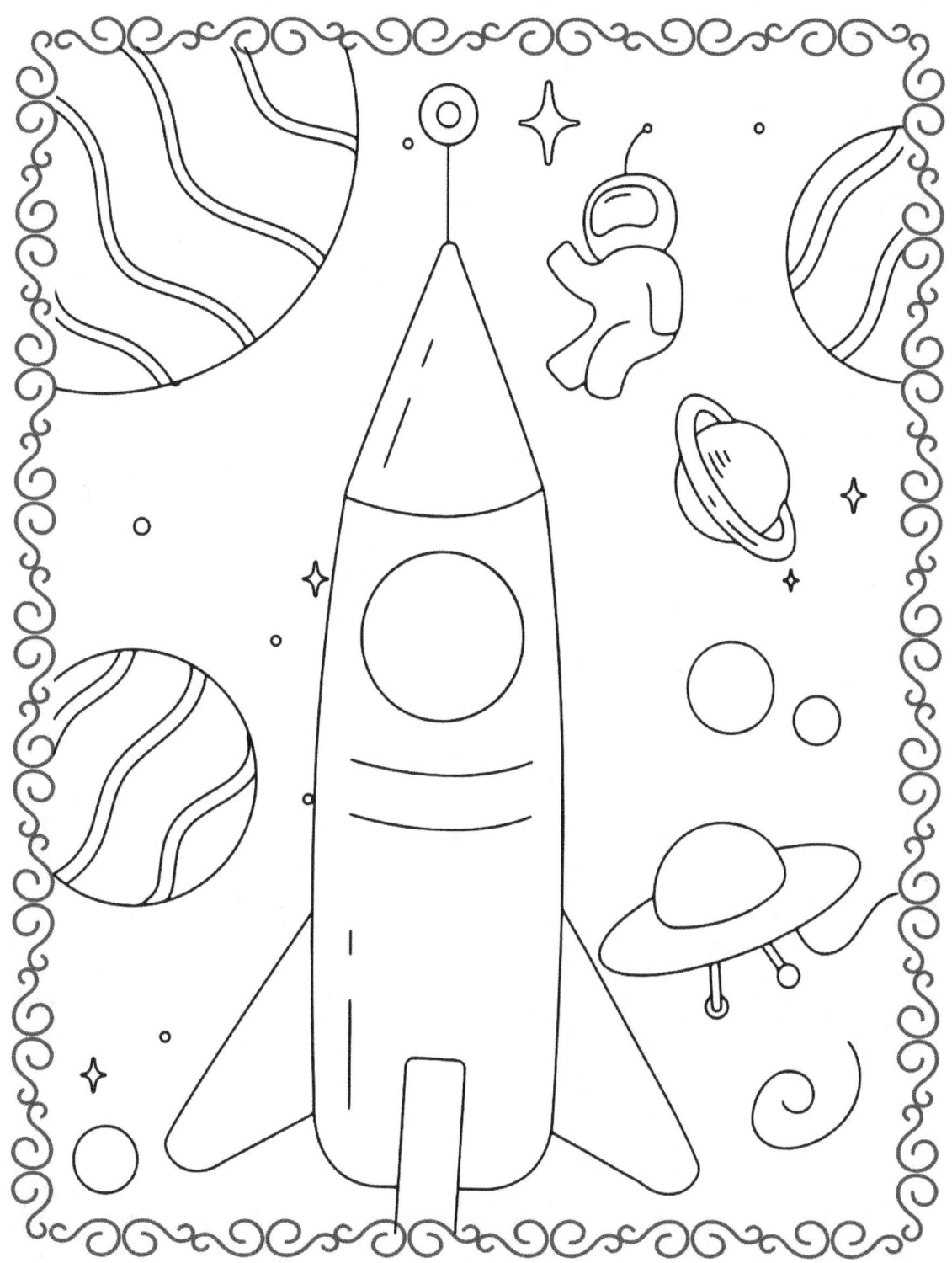

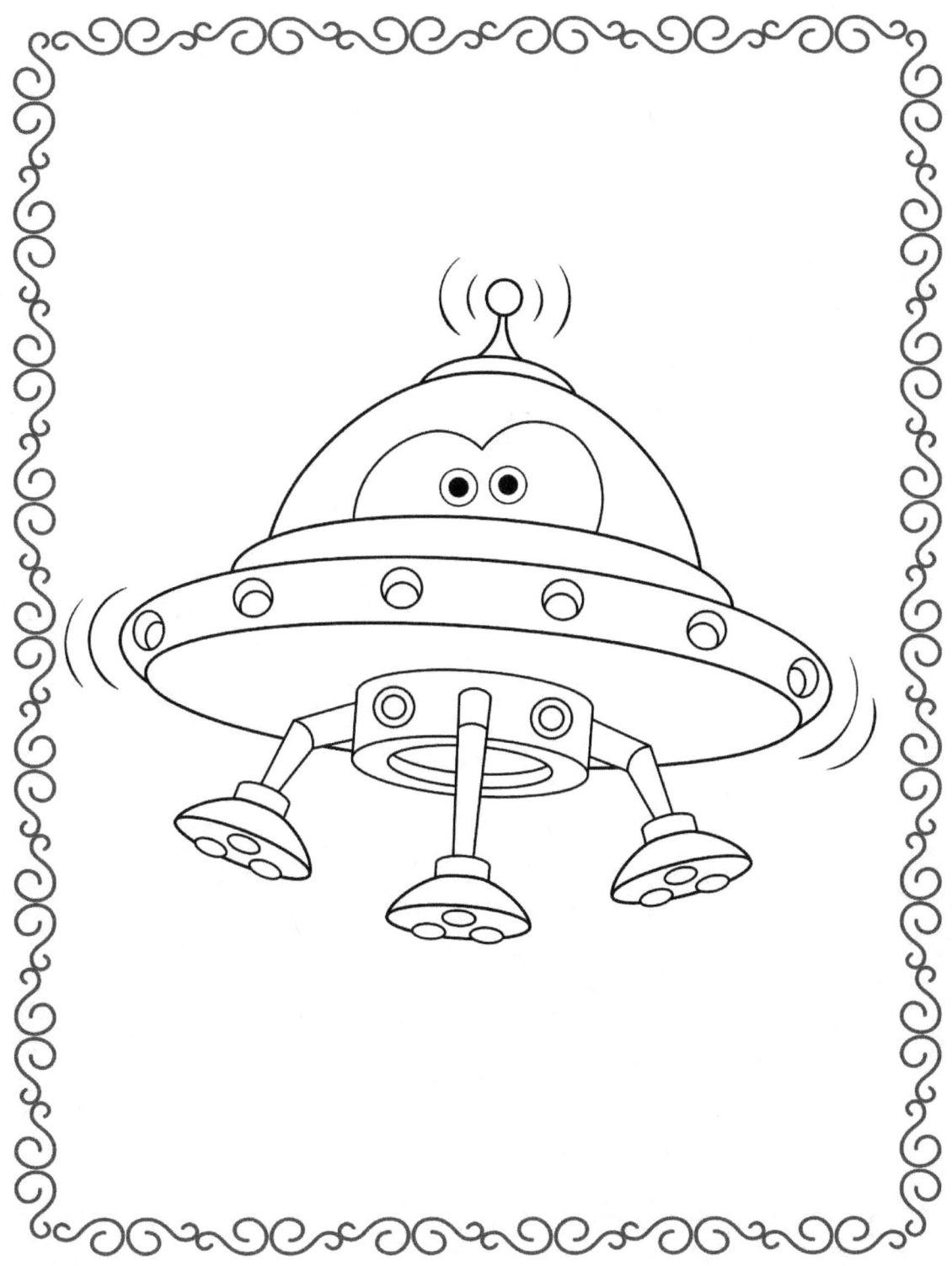

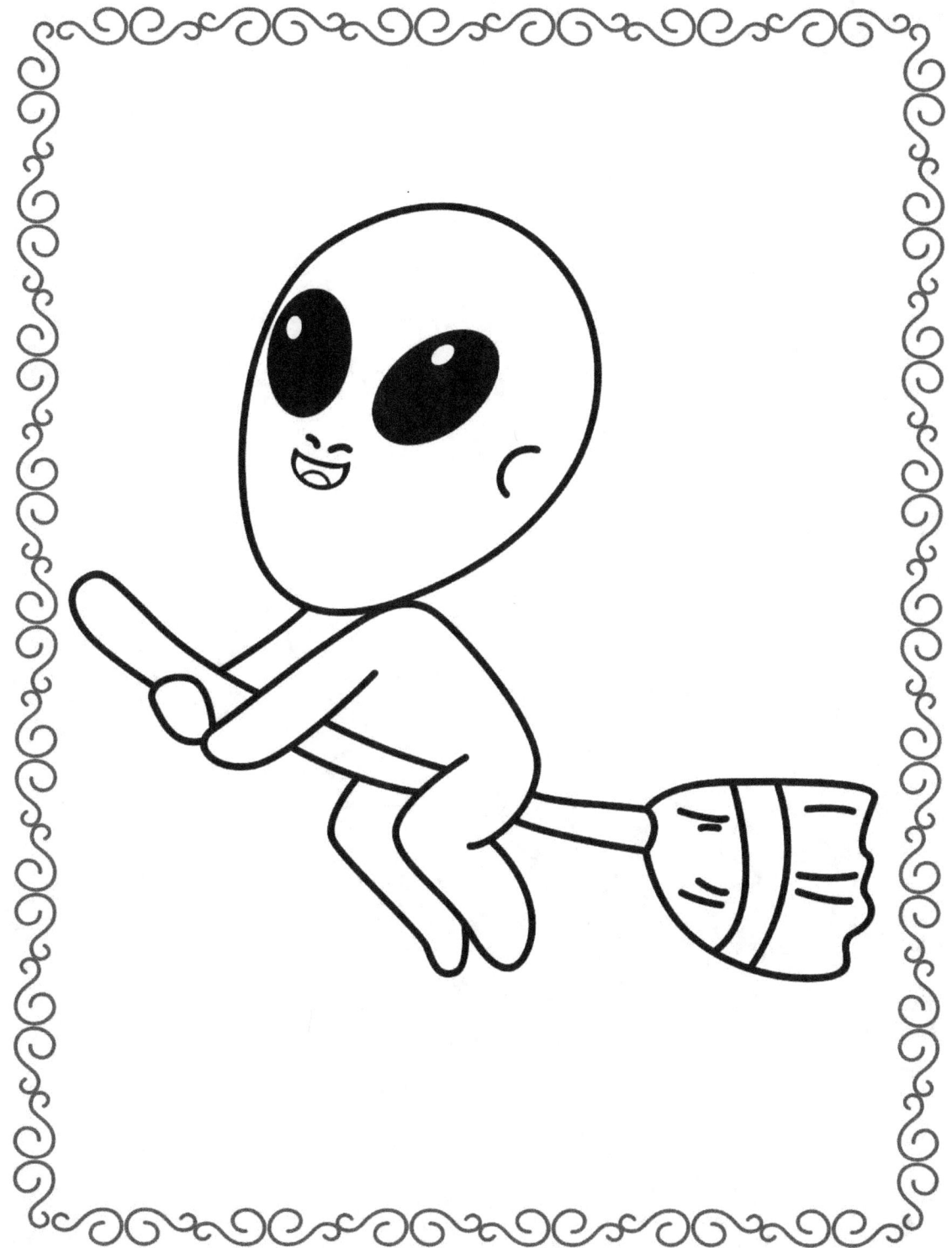

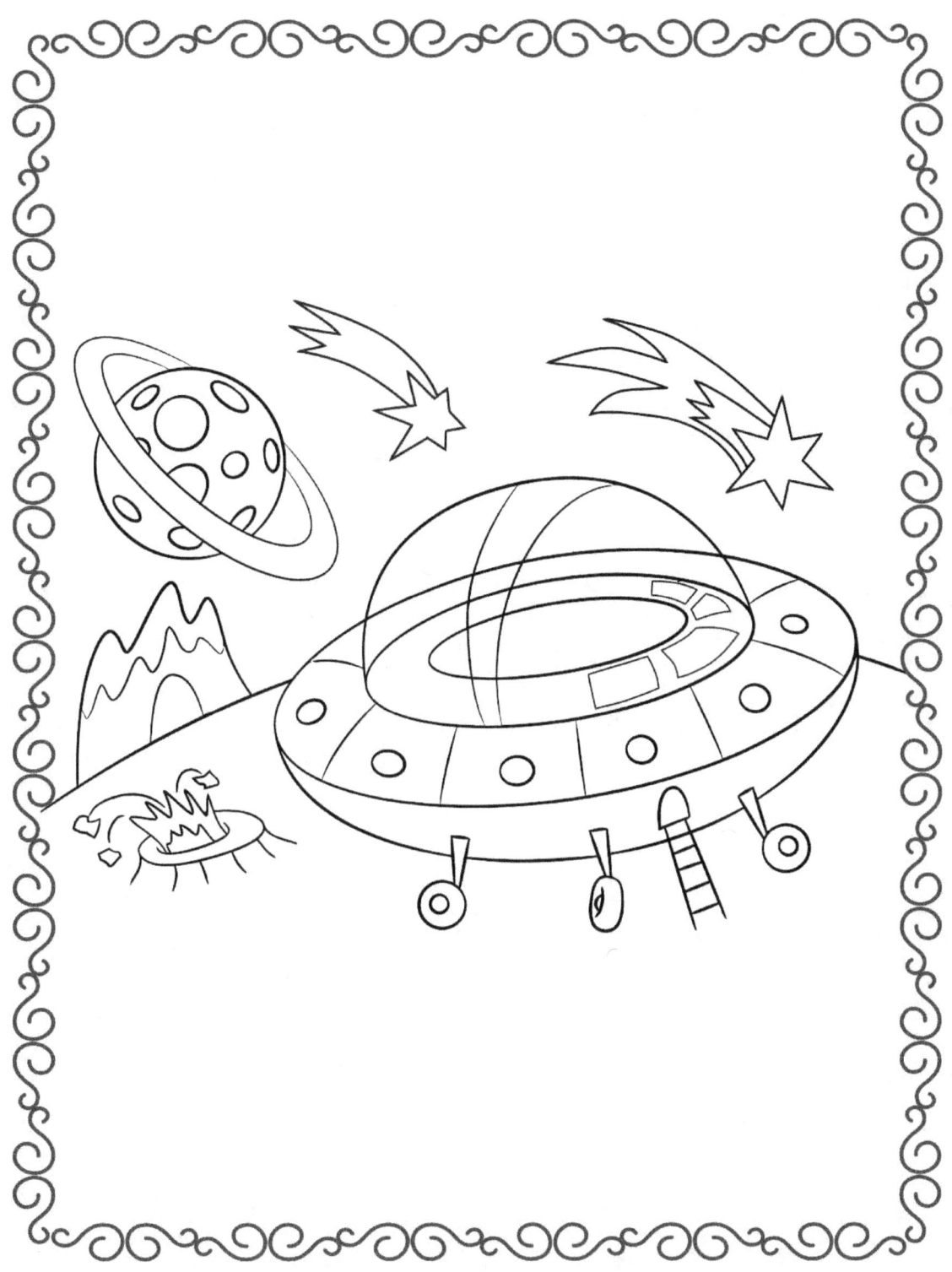

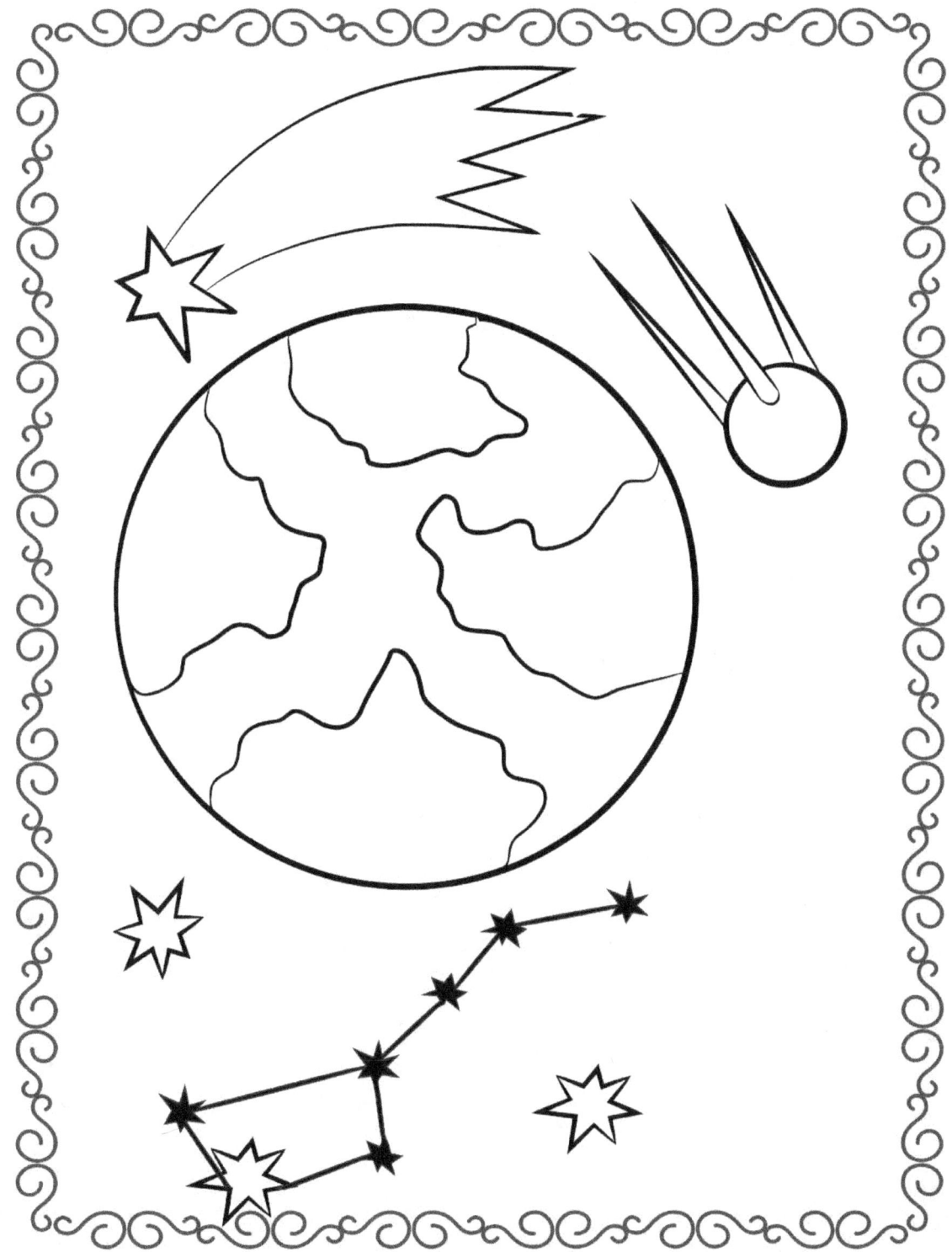

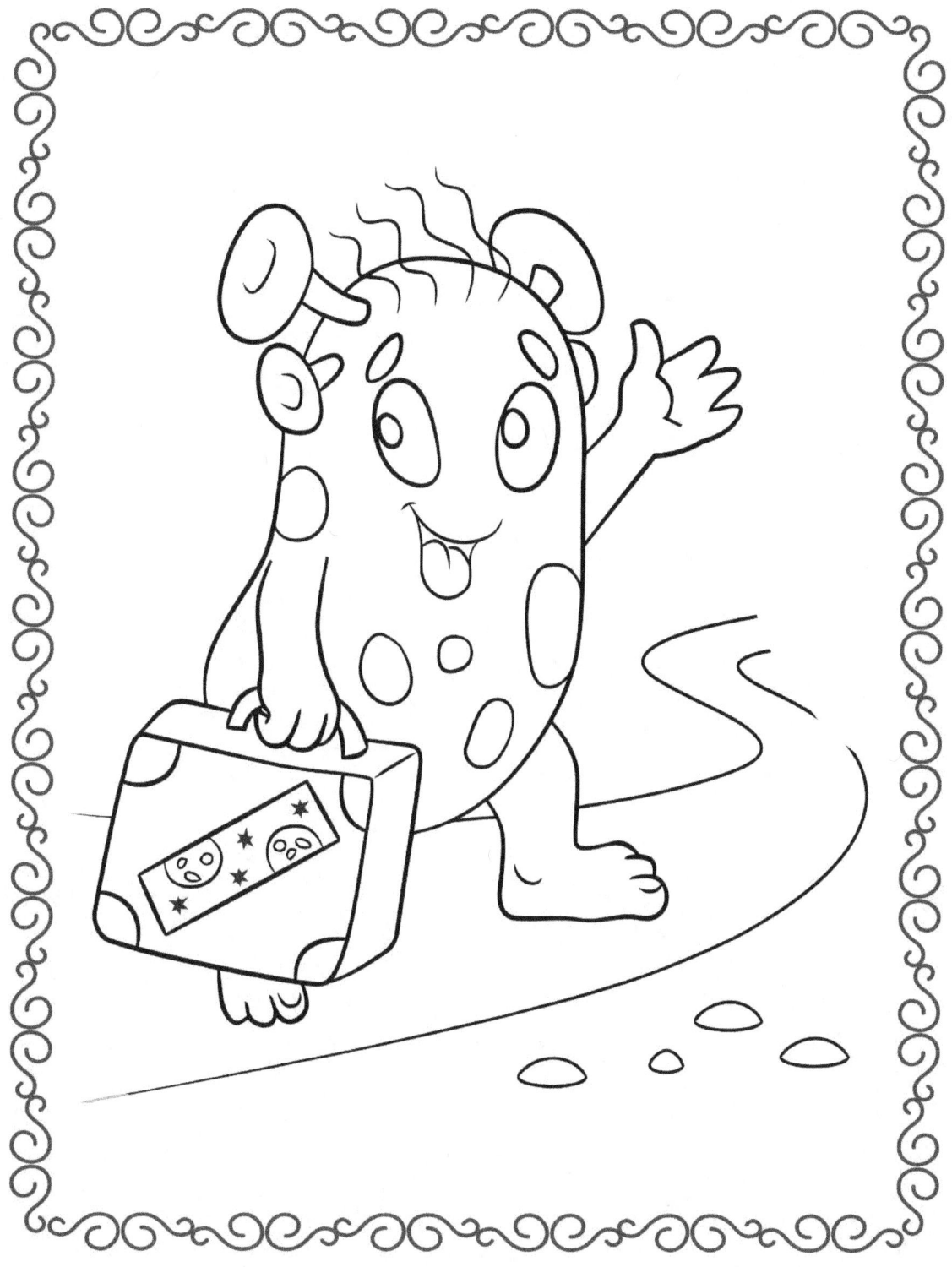

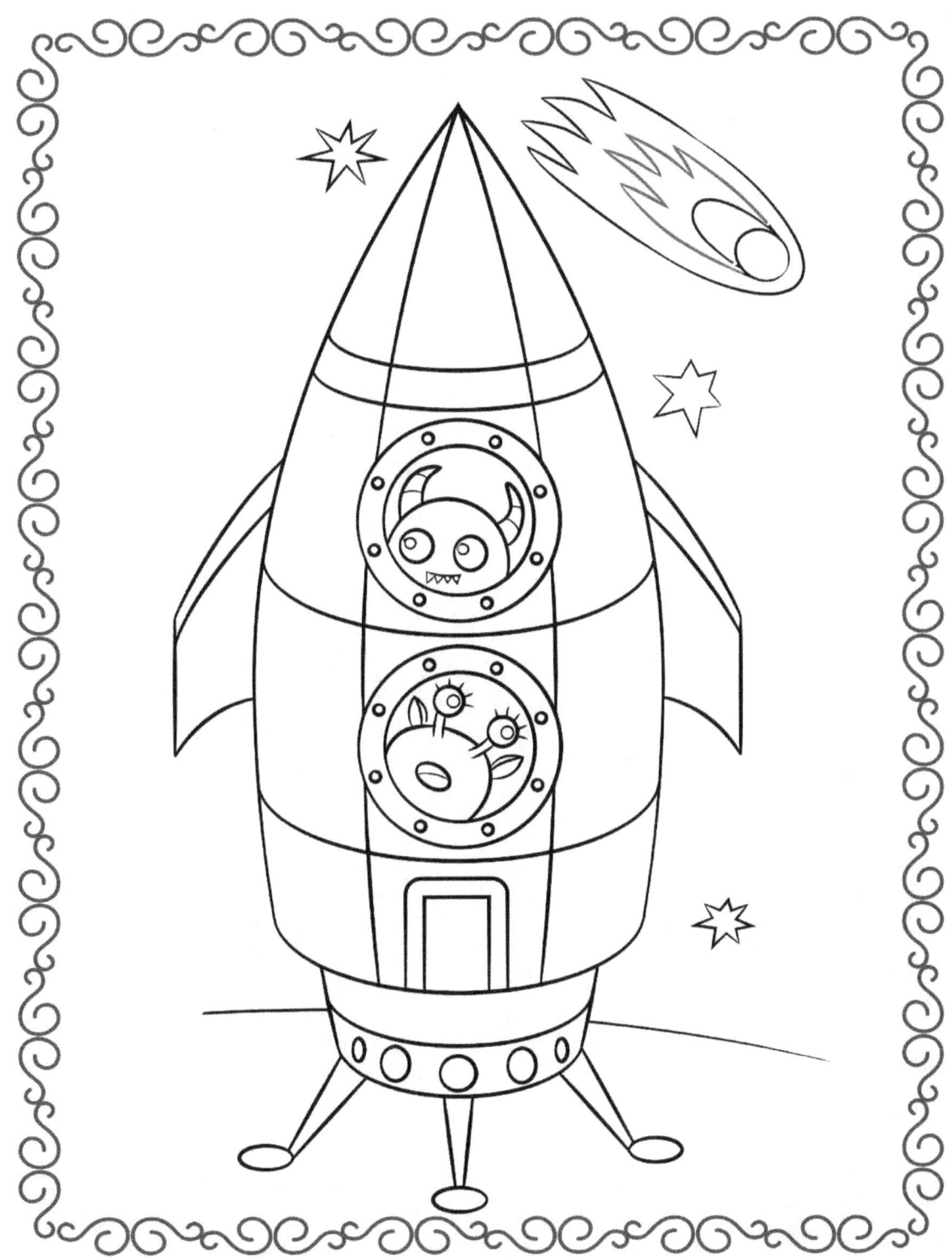

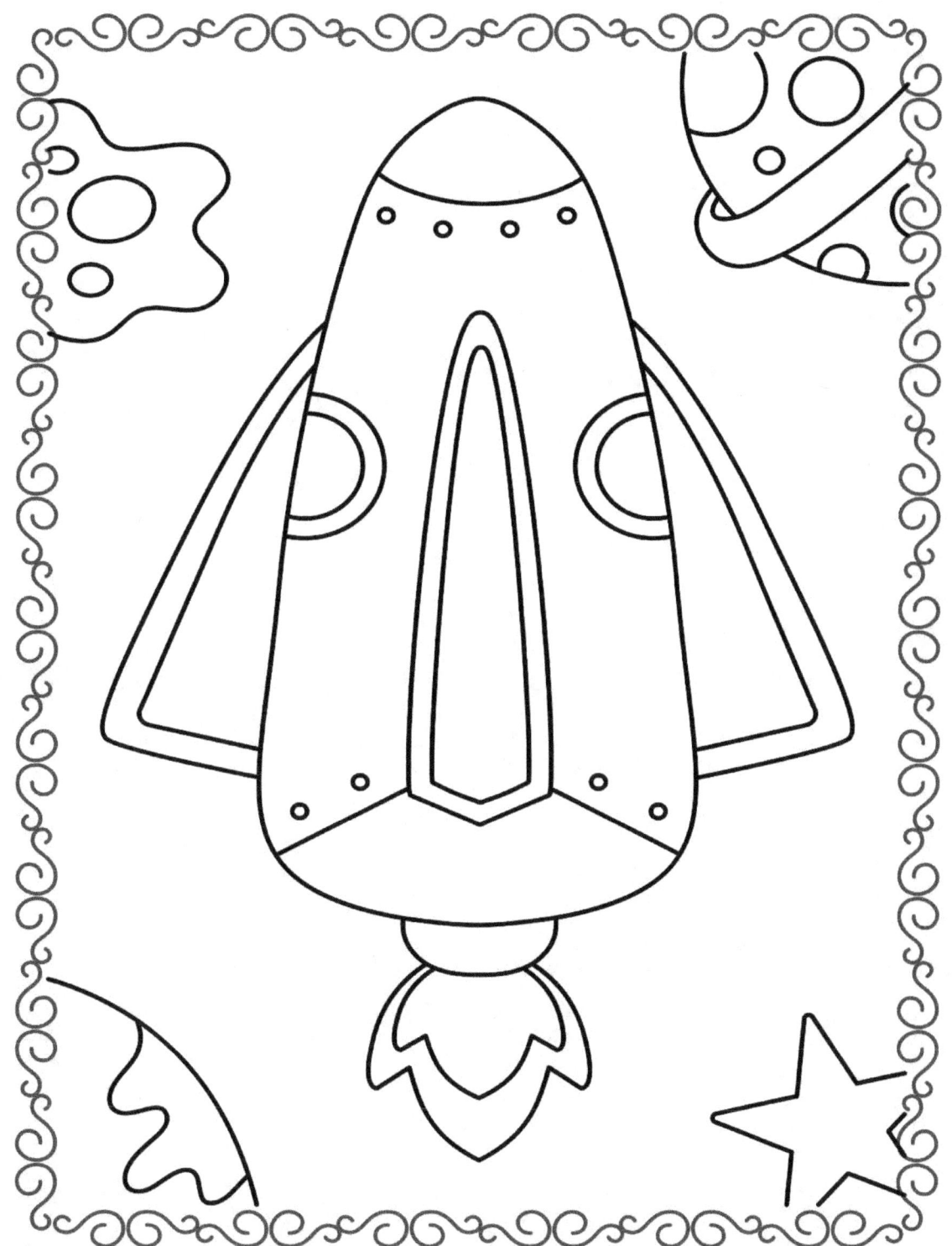

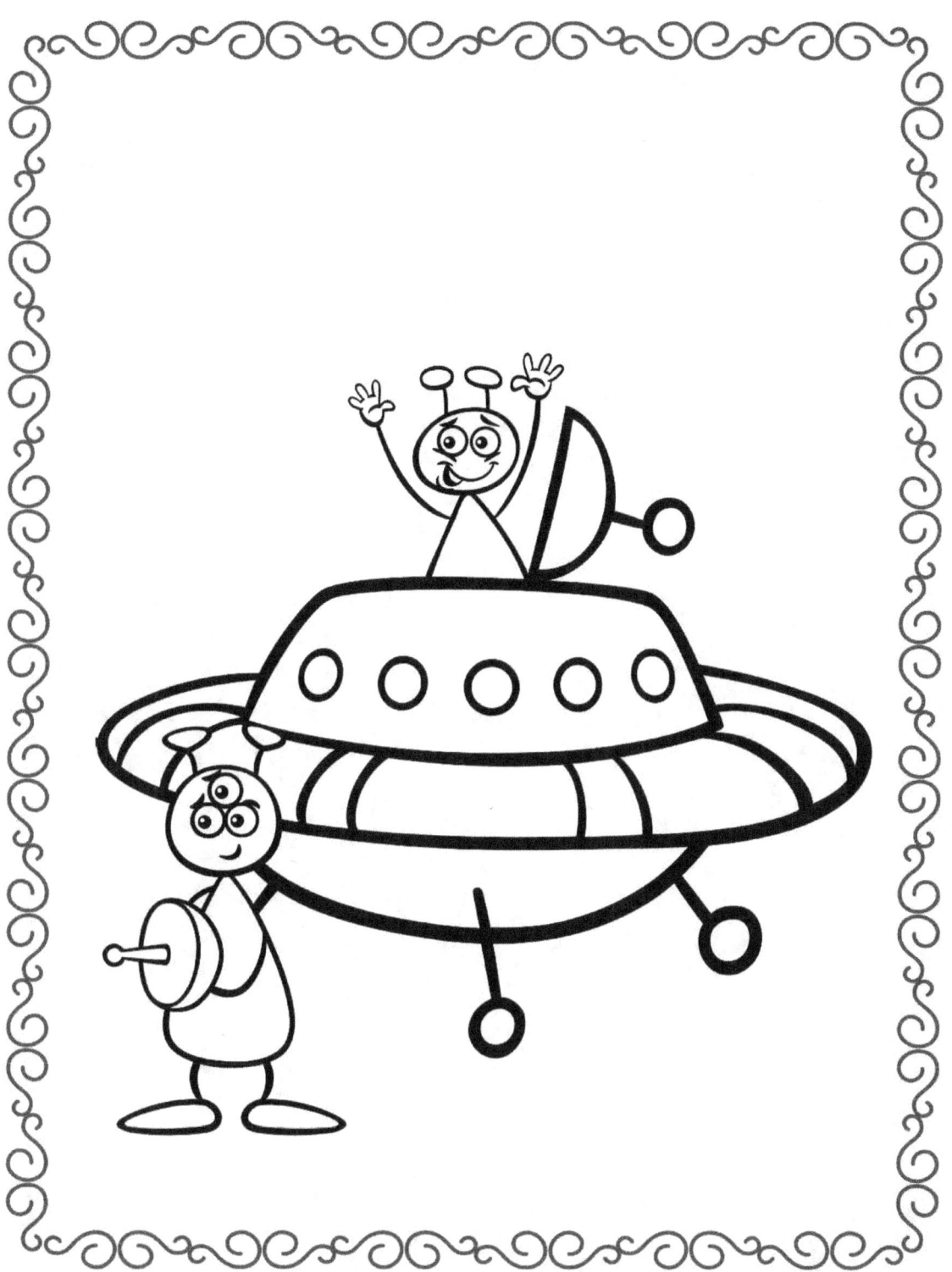

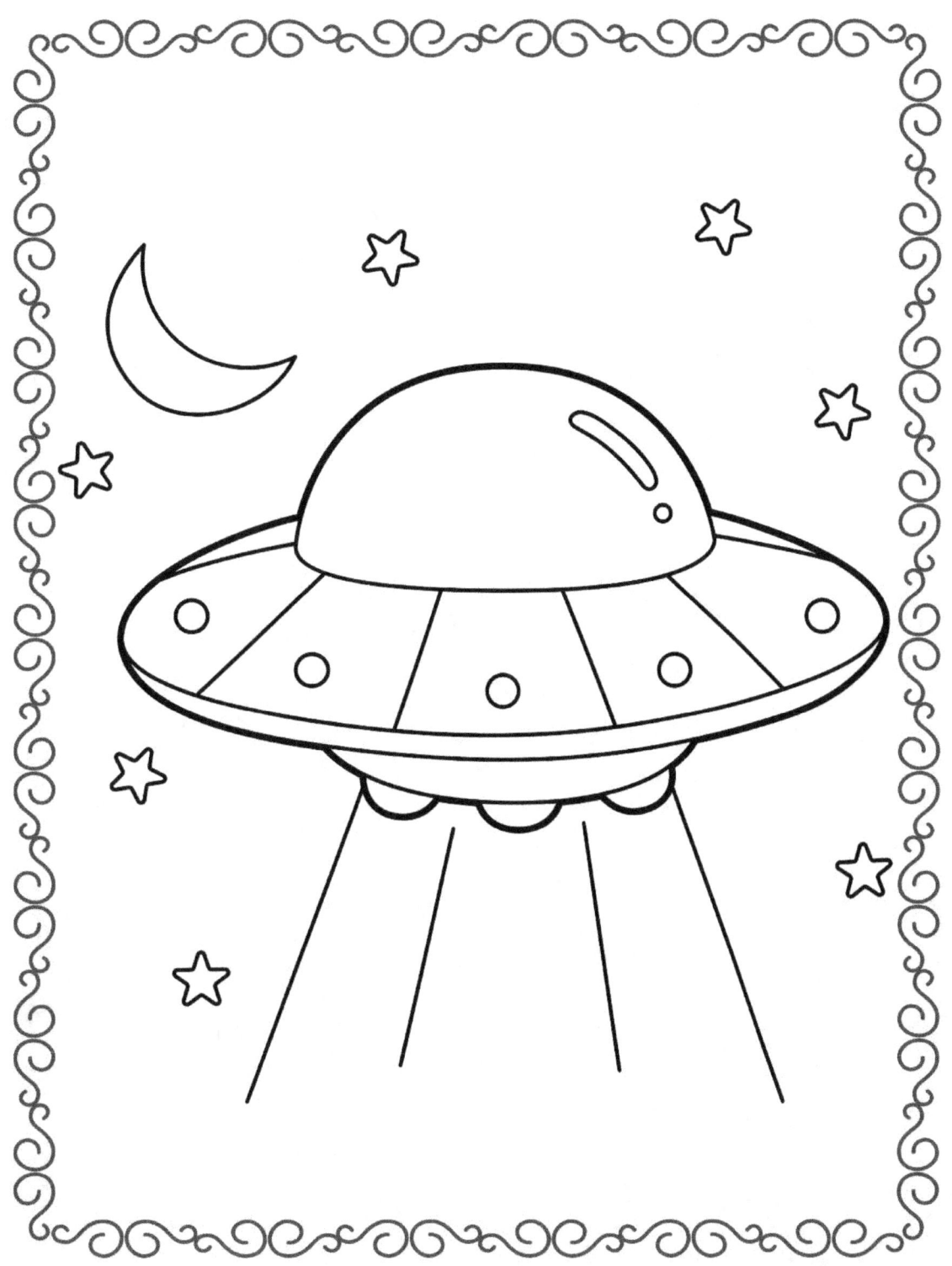

BONUS PAGES

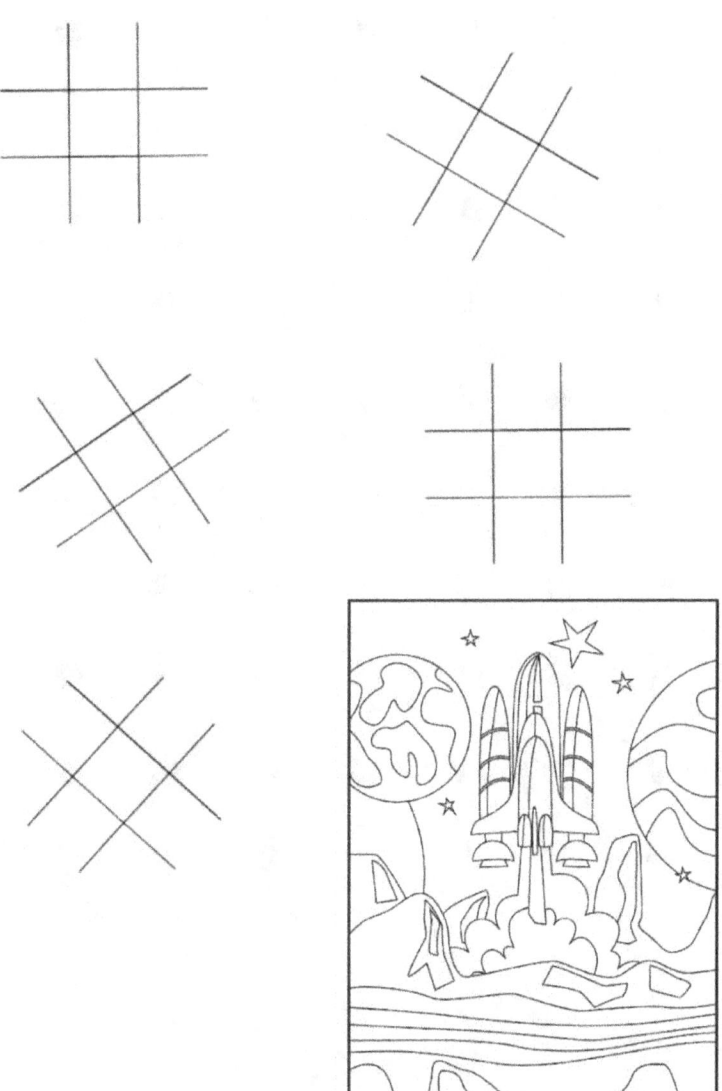

The Dot Game

Take turns connecting the dots until you make a square. Put your initials in each square. At the end, the person with the most squares win.

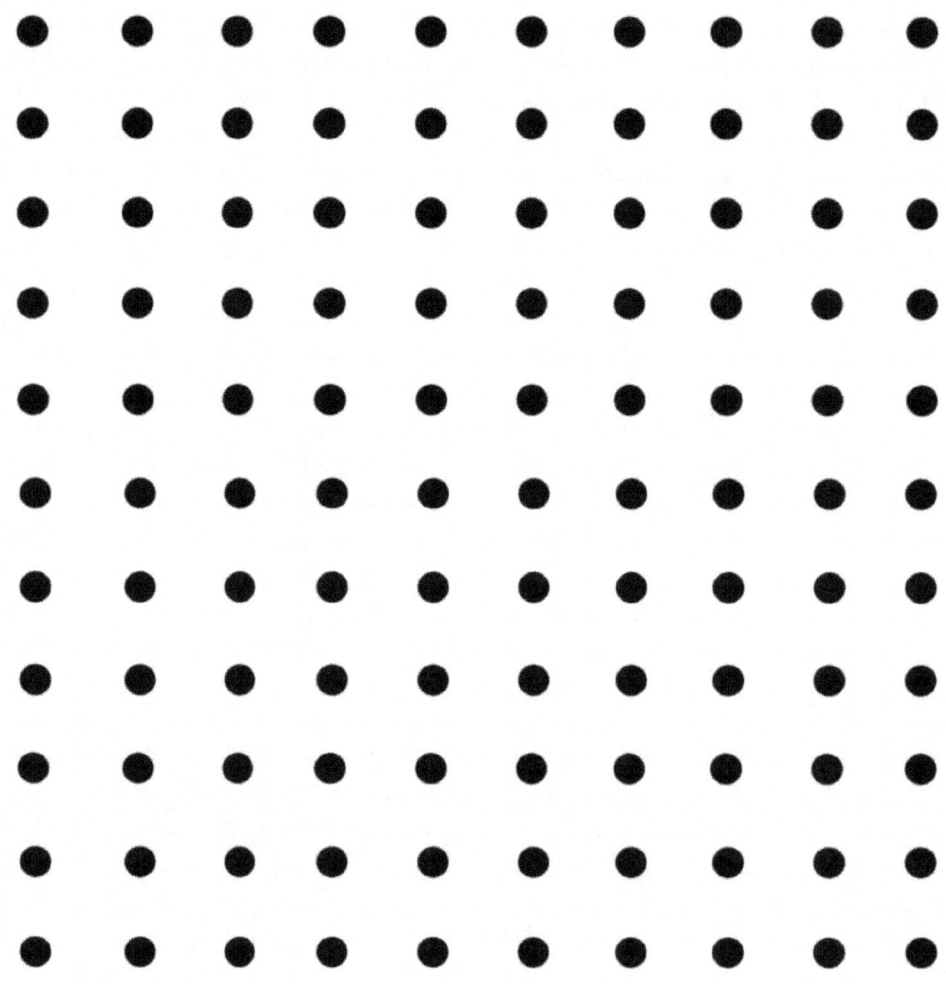

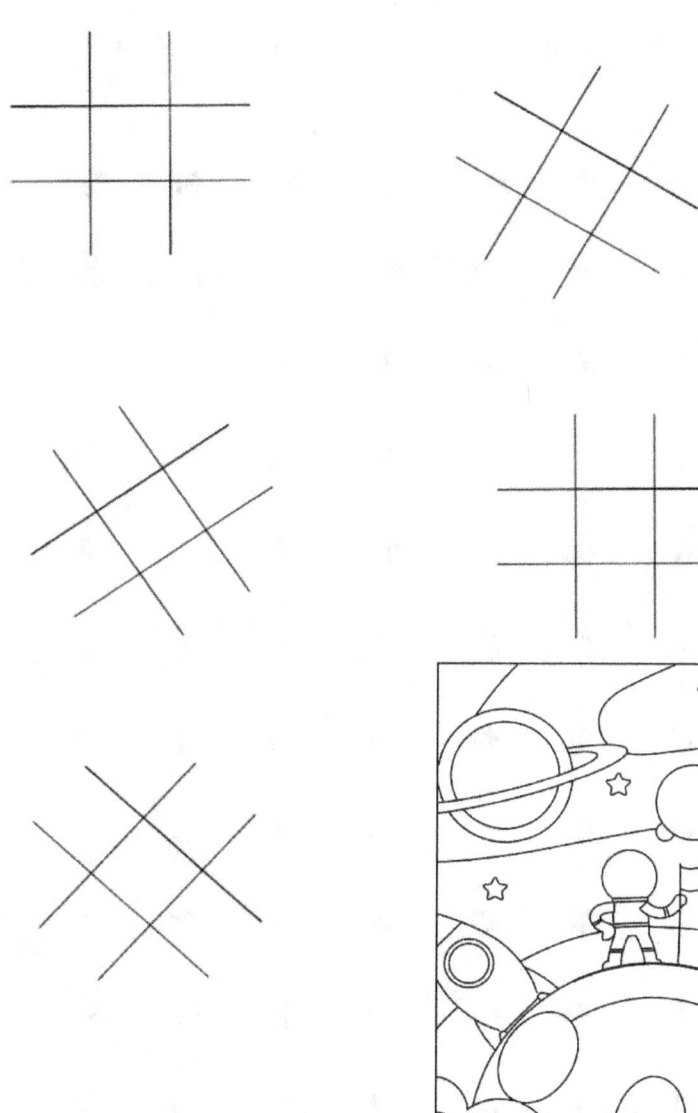

The Dot Game
Take turns connecting the dots until you make a square. Put your initials in each square. At the end, the person with the most squares win.

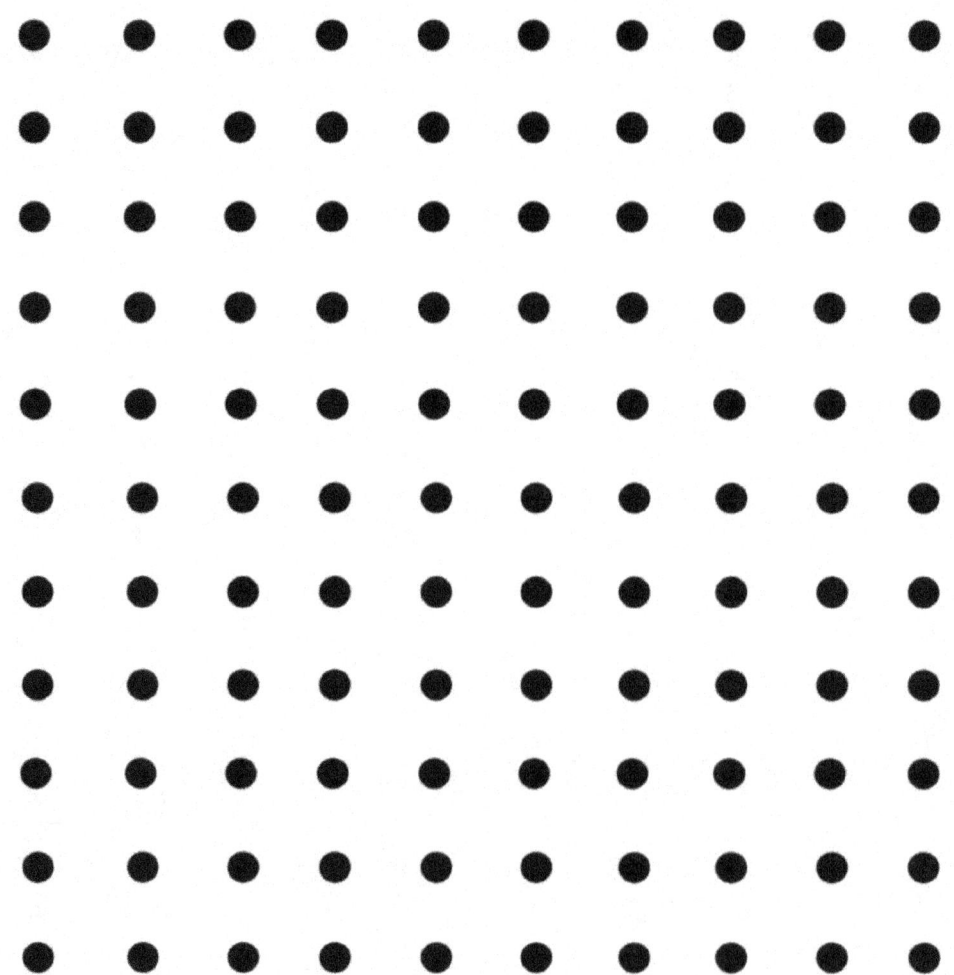

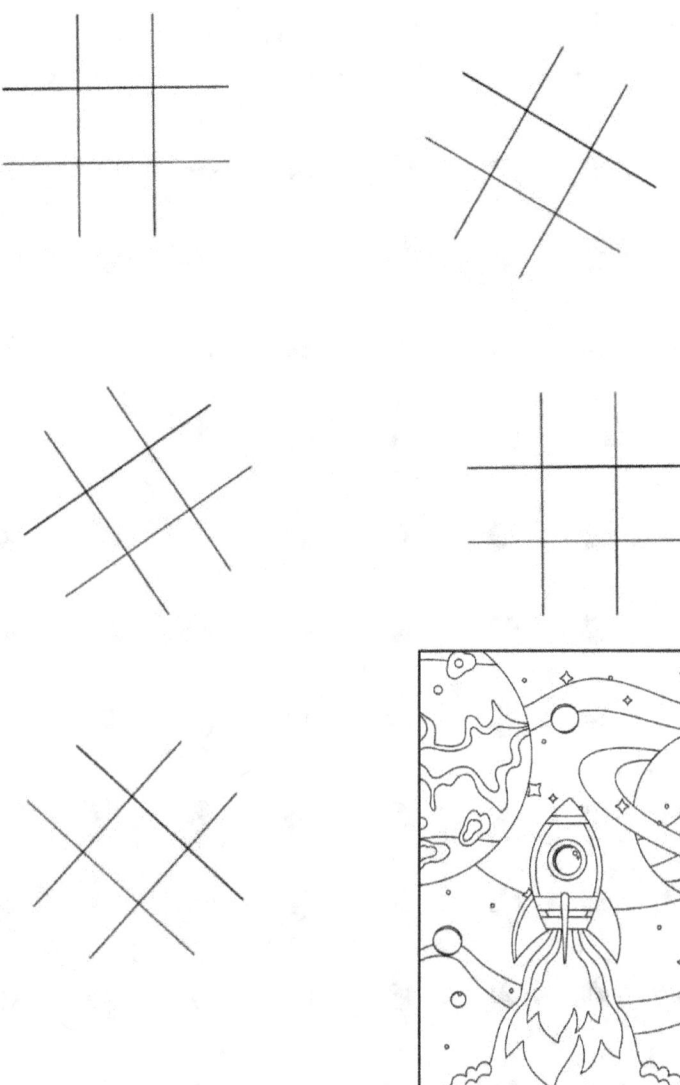

The Dot Game

Take turns connecting the dots until you make a square. Put your initials in each square. At the end, the person with the most squares win.

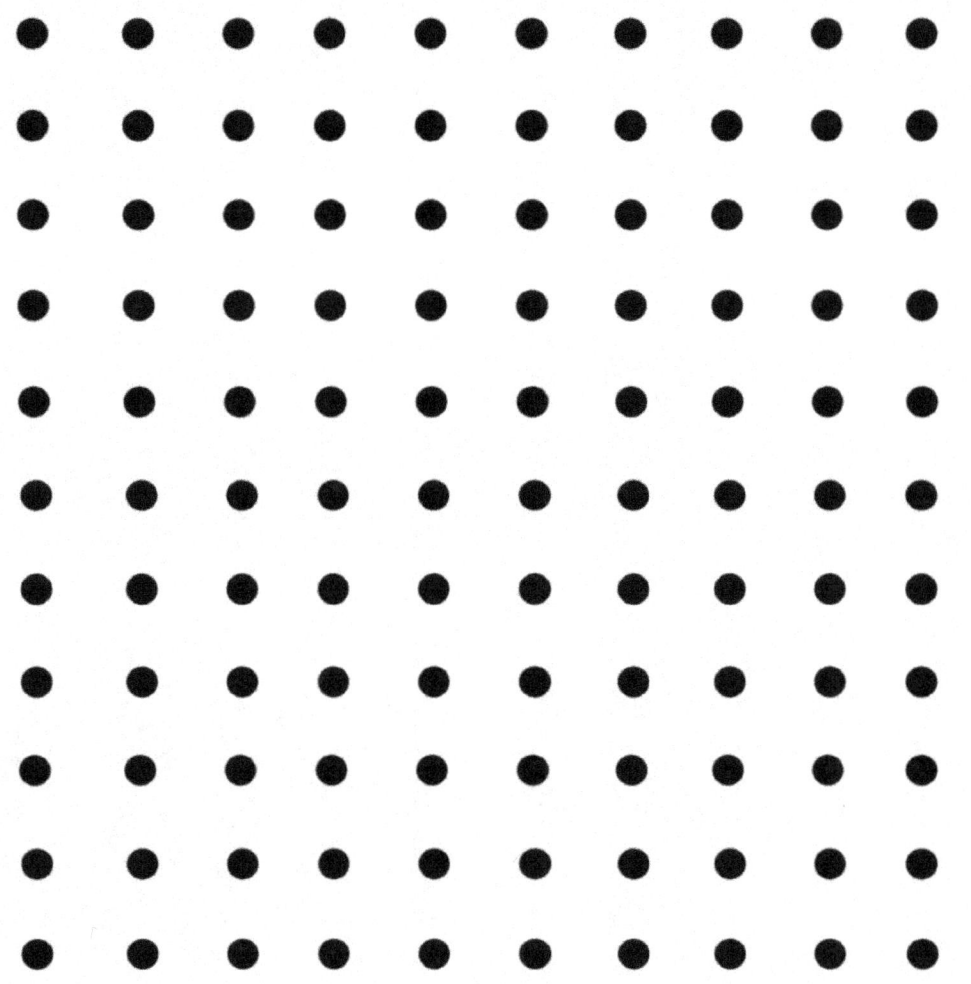

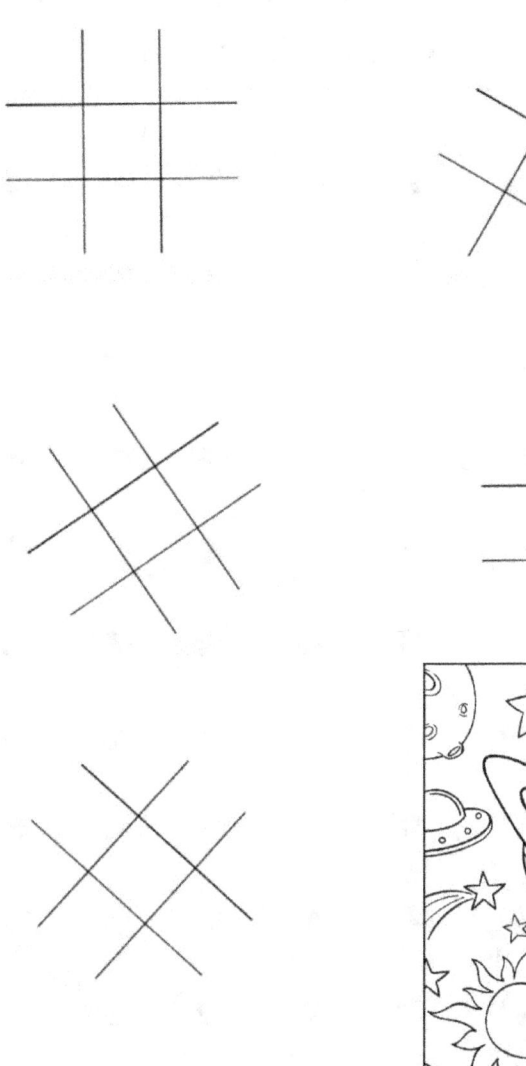

The Dot Game

Take turns connecting the dots until you make a square. Put your initials in each square. At the end, the person with the most squares win.

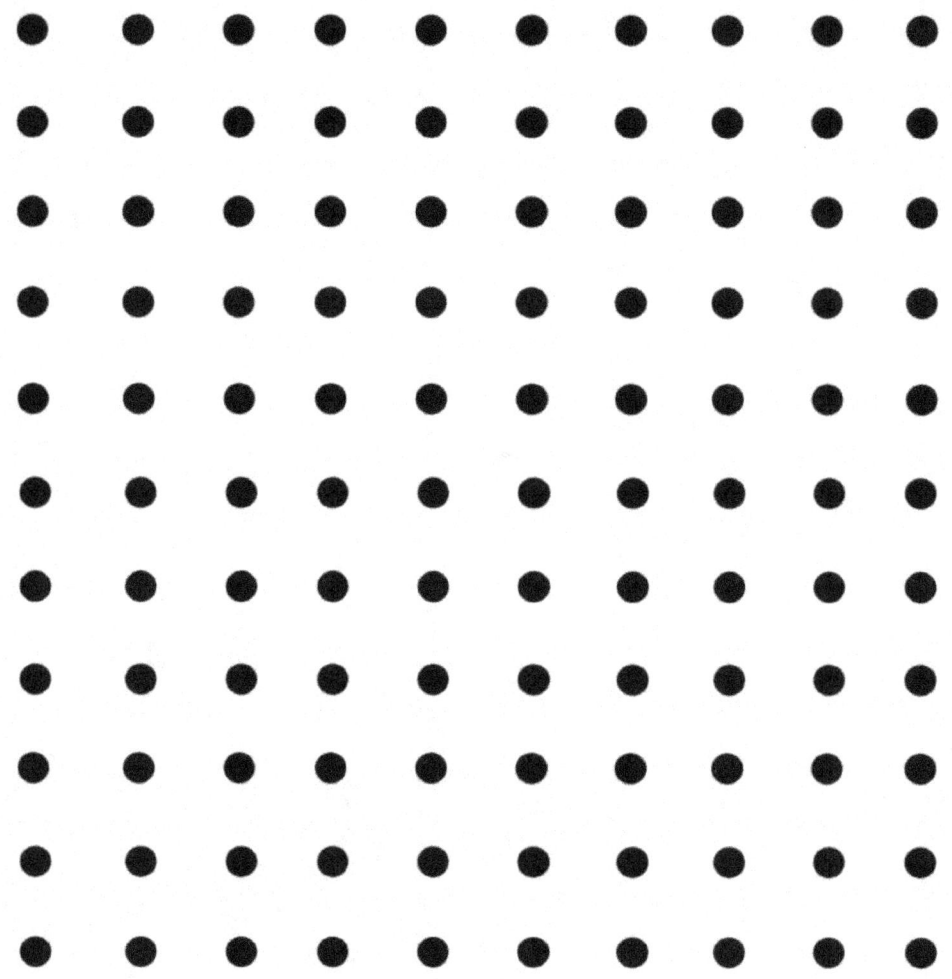

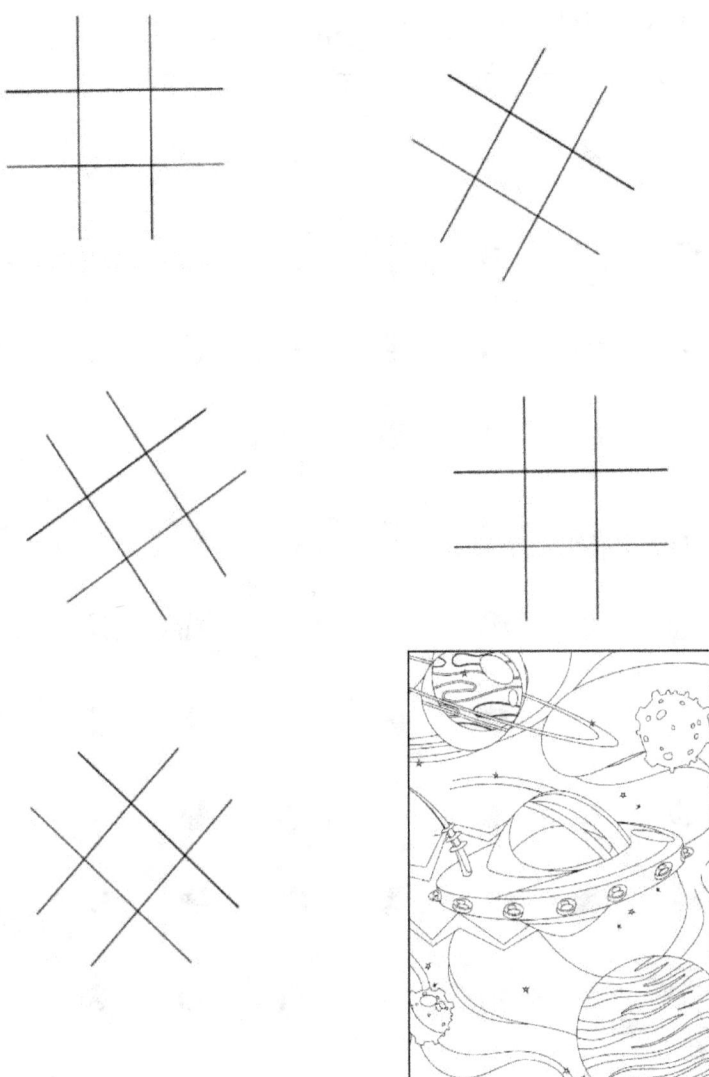

The Dot Game
Take turns connecting the dots until you make a square. Put your initials in each square. At the end, the person with the most squares win.

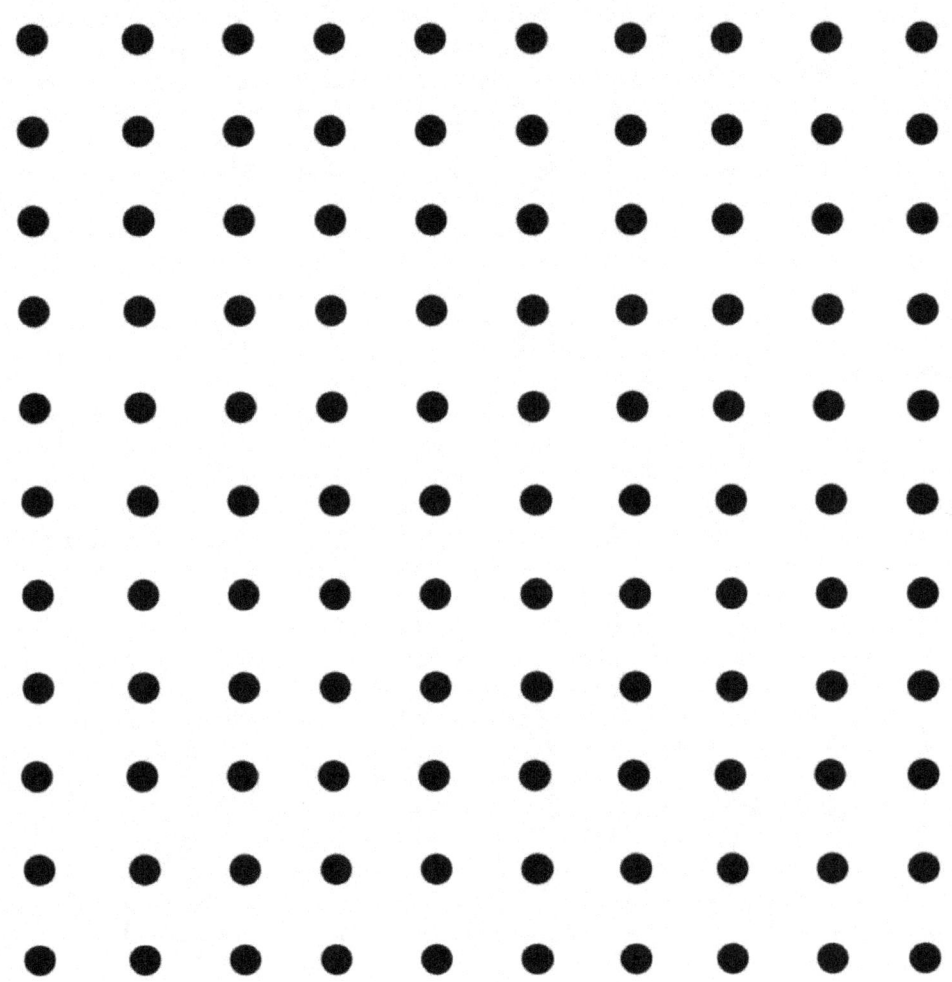

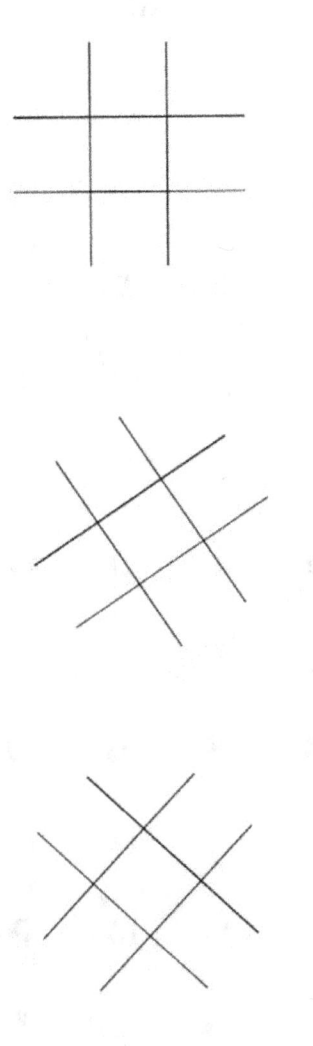
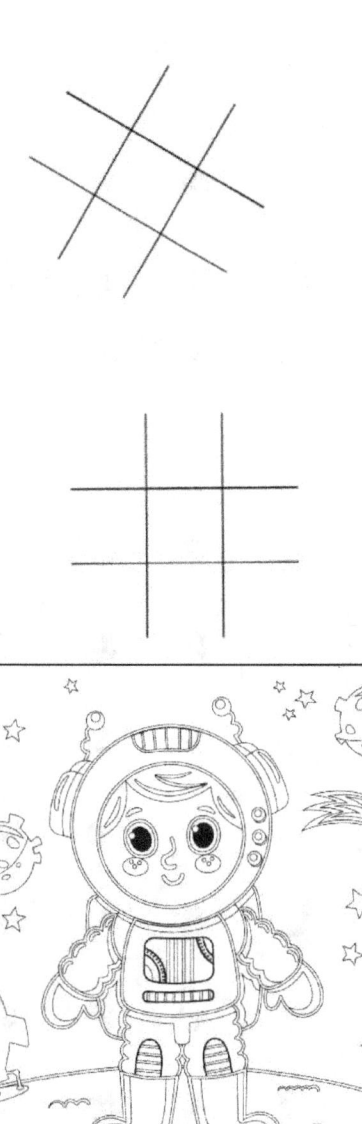

The Dot Game

Take turns connecting the dots until you make a square. Put your initials in each square. At the end, the person with the most squares win.

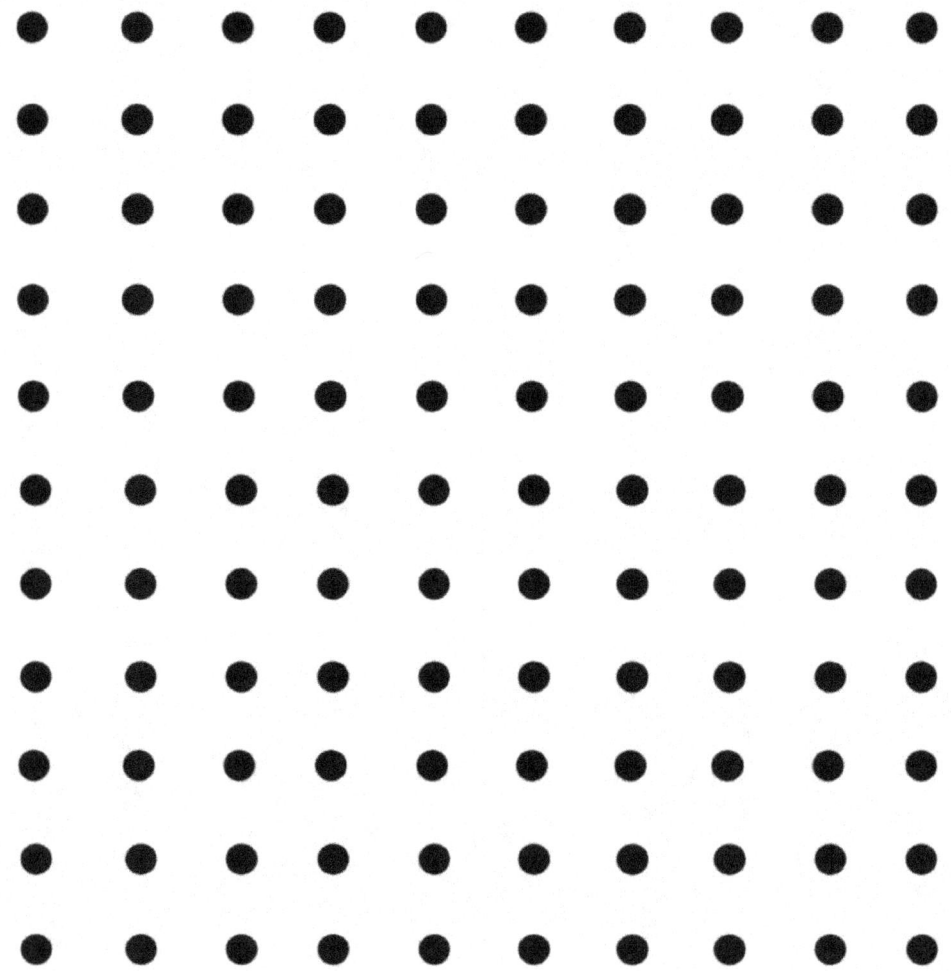

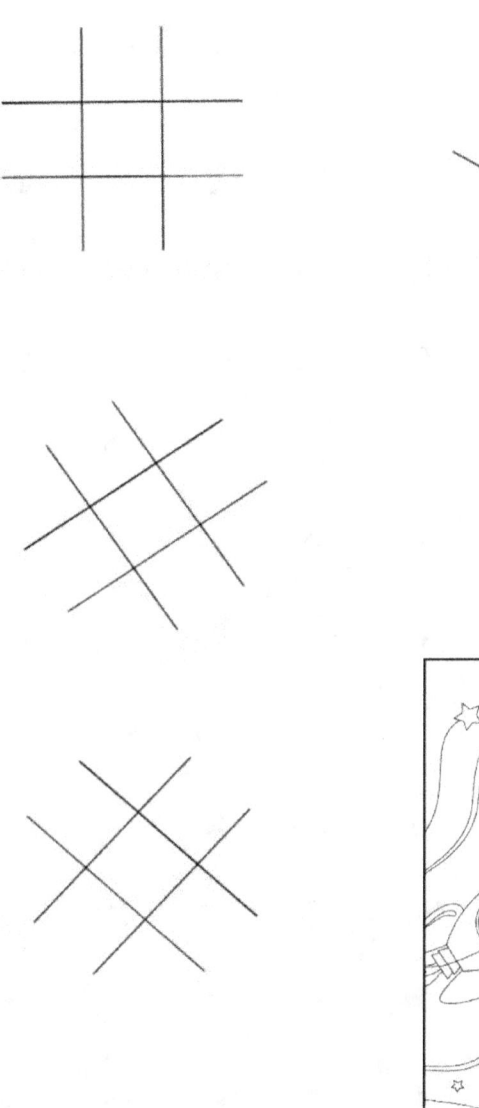
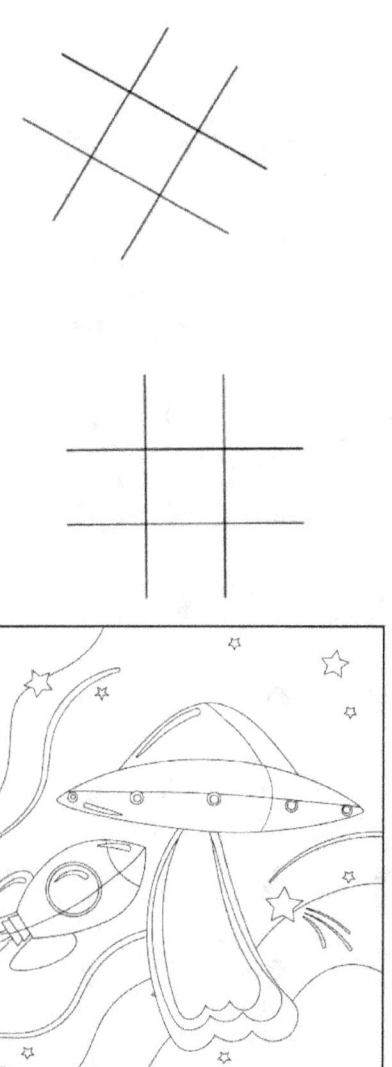

The Dot Game

Take turns connecting the dots until you make a square. Put your initials in each square. At the end, the person with the most squares win.

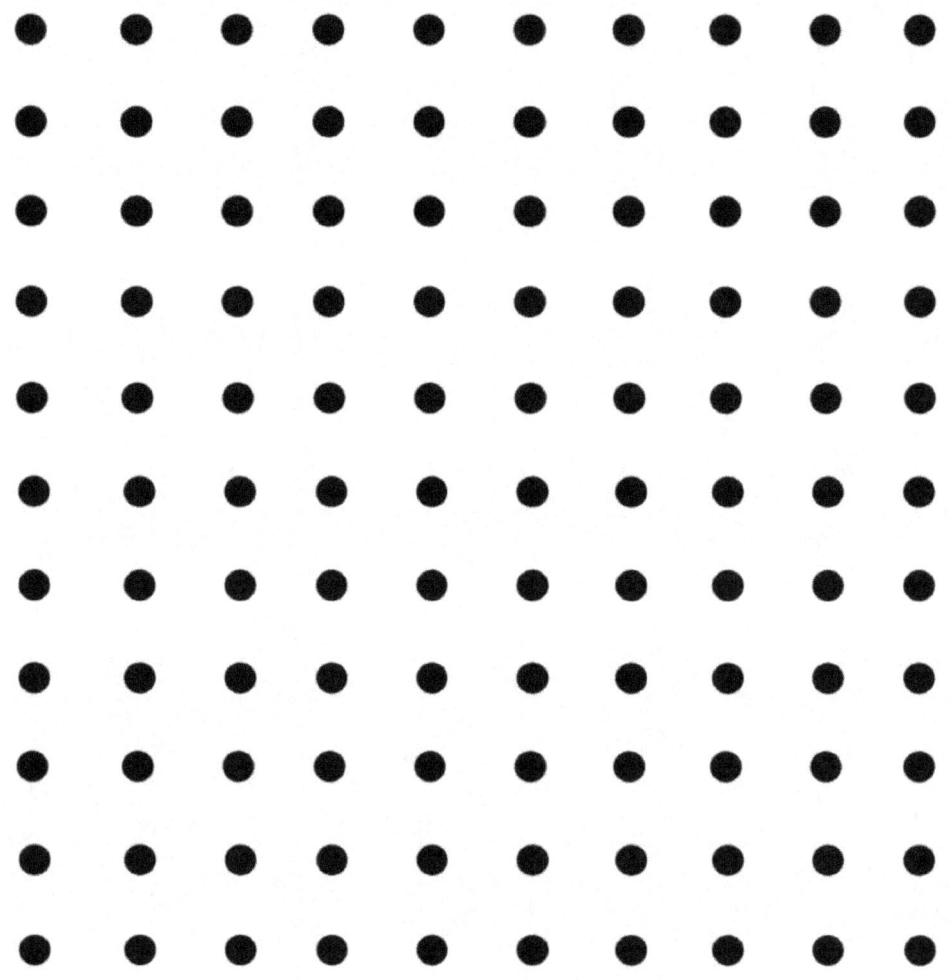

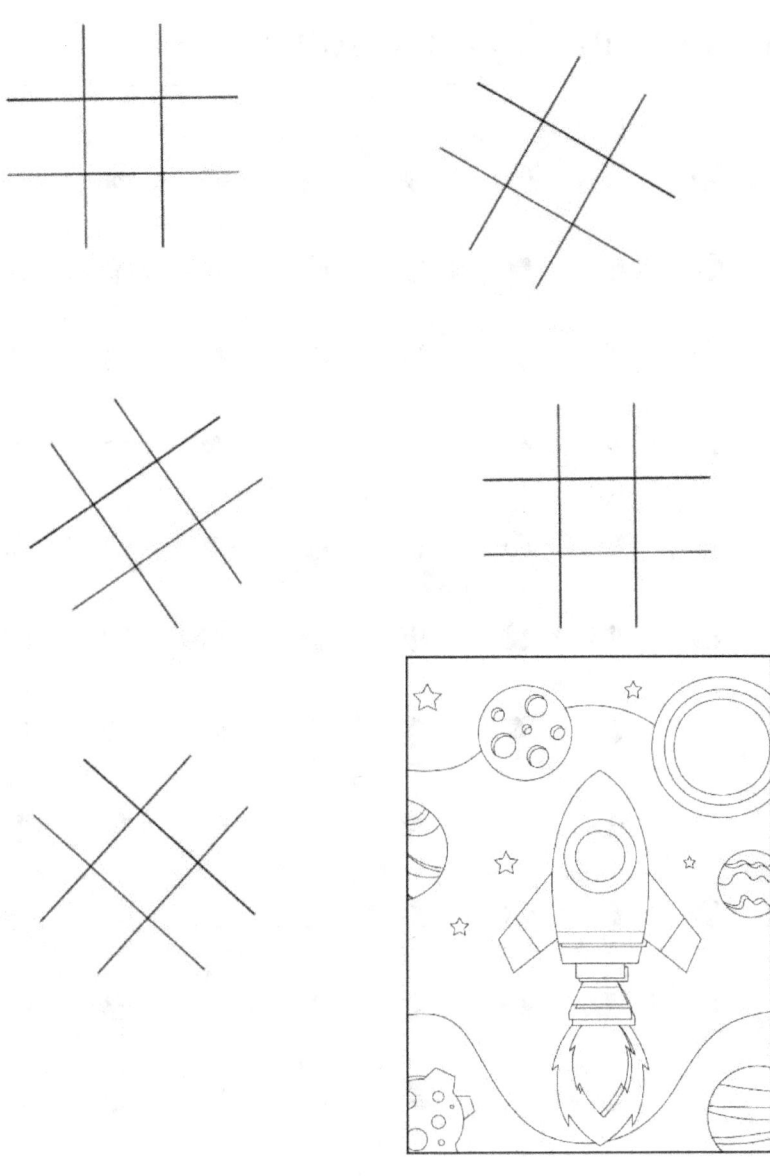

The Dot Game

Take turns connecting the dots until you make a square. Put your initials in each square. At the end, the person with the most squares win.

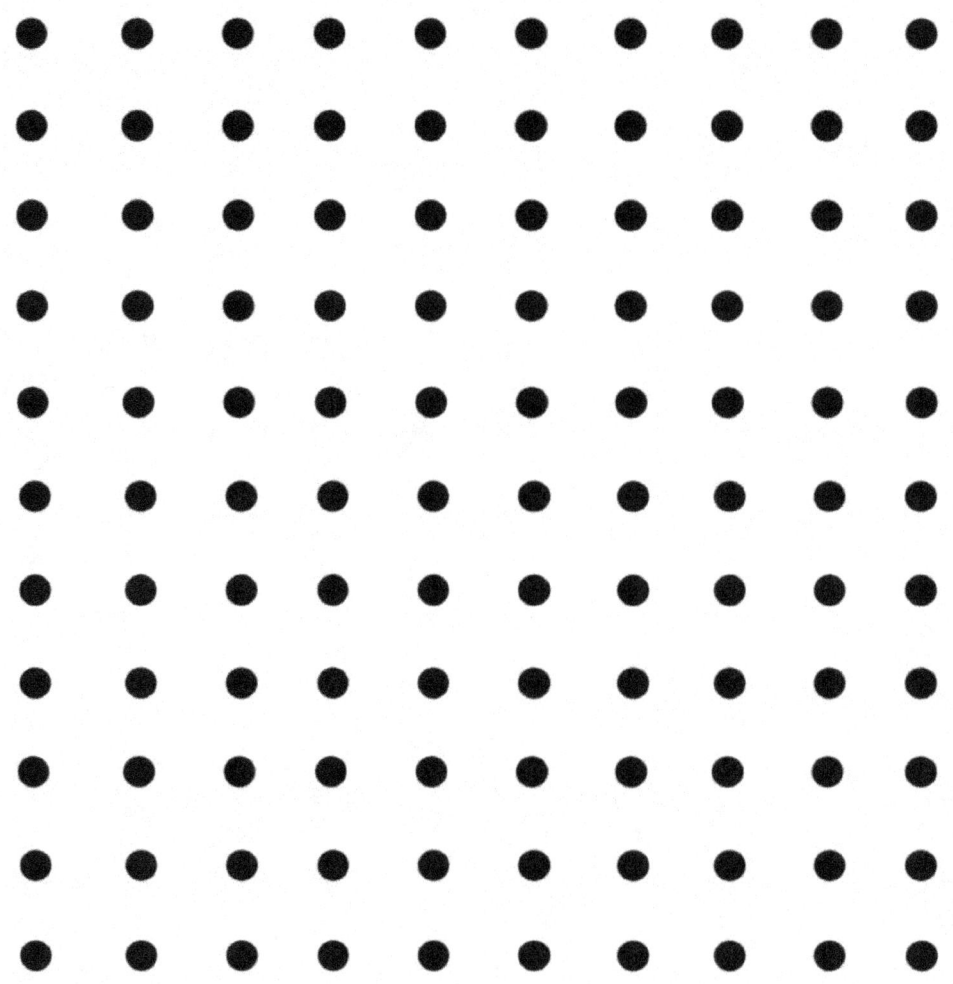

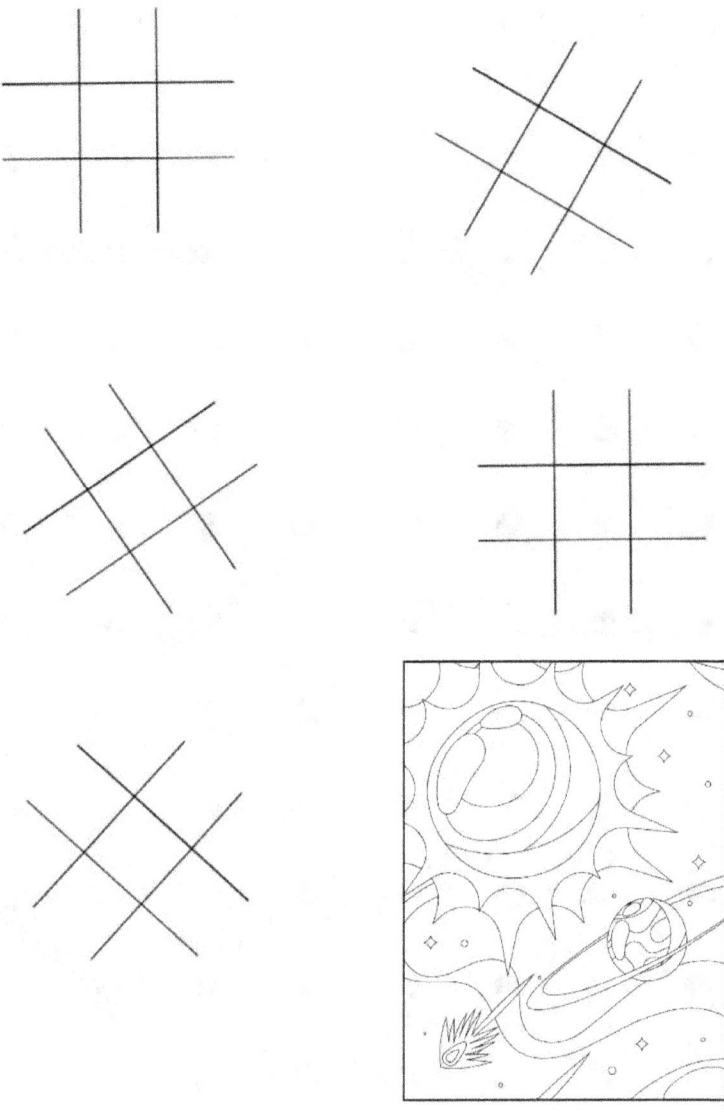

The Dot Game

Take turns connecting the dots until you make a square. Put your initials in each square. At the end, the person with the most squares win.

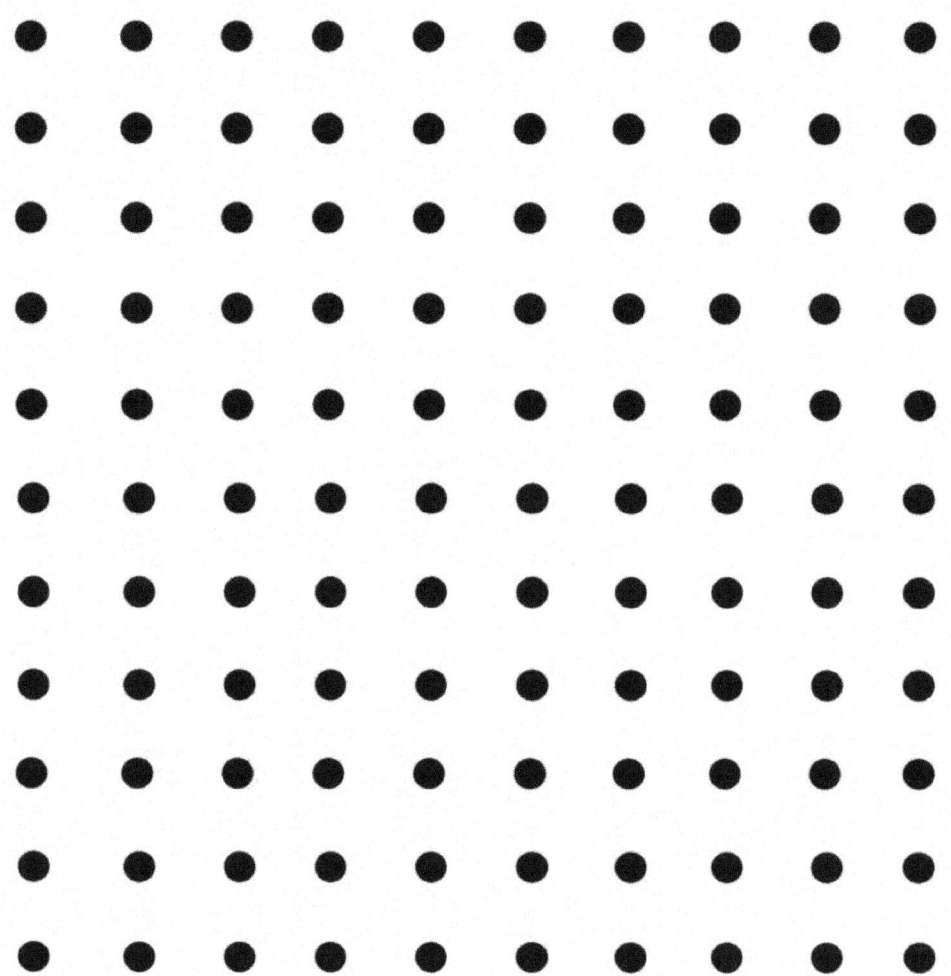

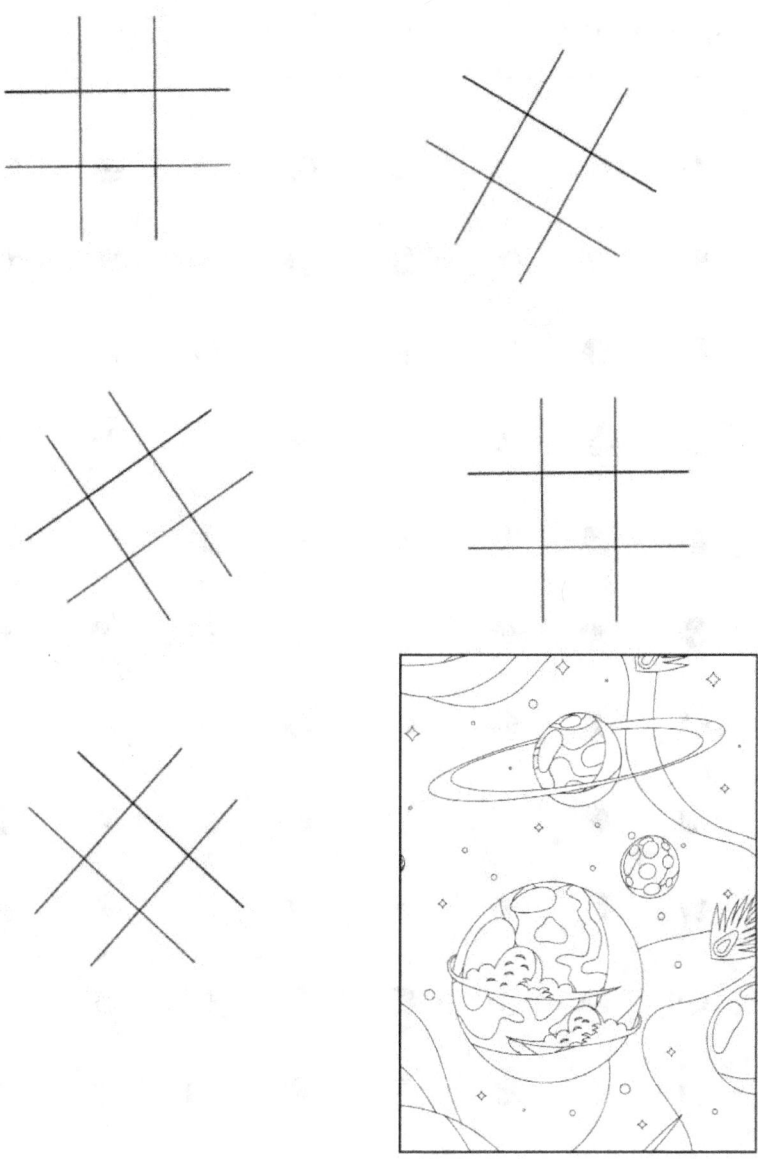

The Dot Game

Take turns connecting the dots until you make a square. Put your initials in each square. At the end, the person with the most squares win.

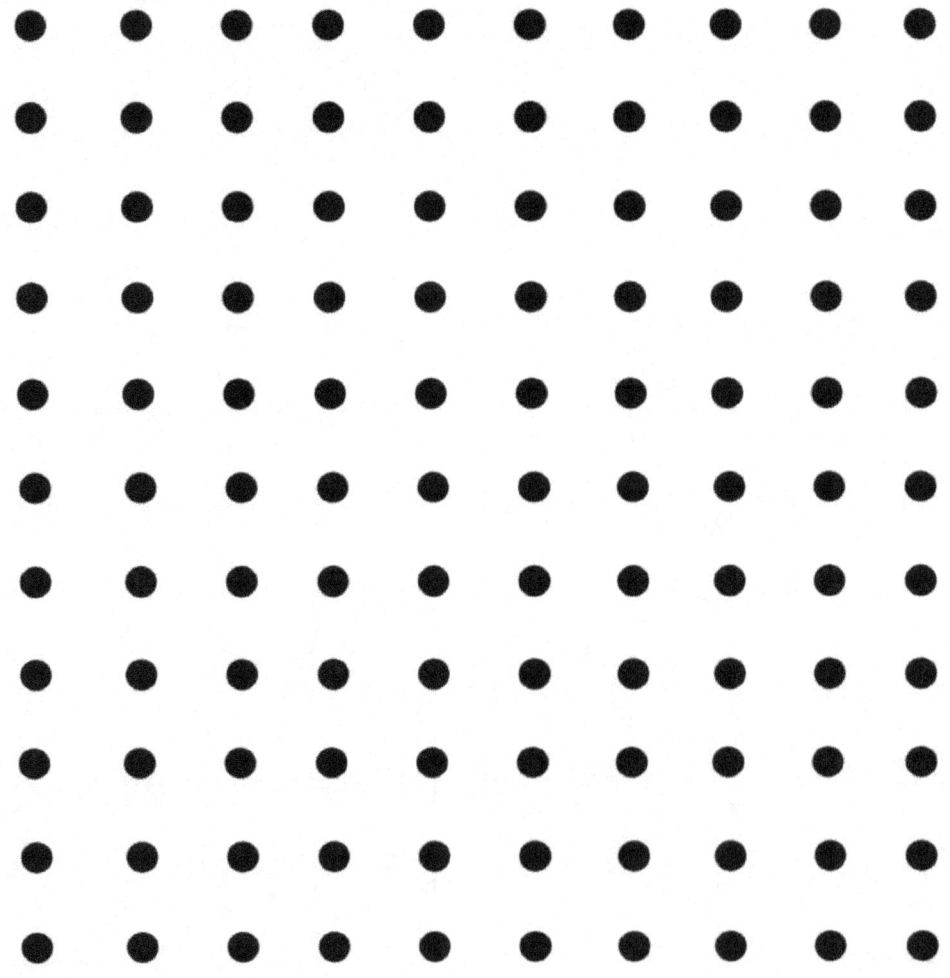

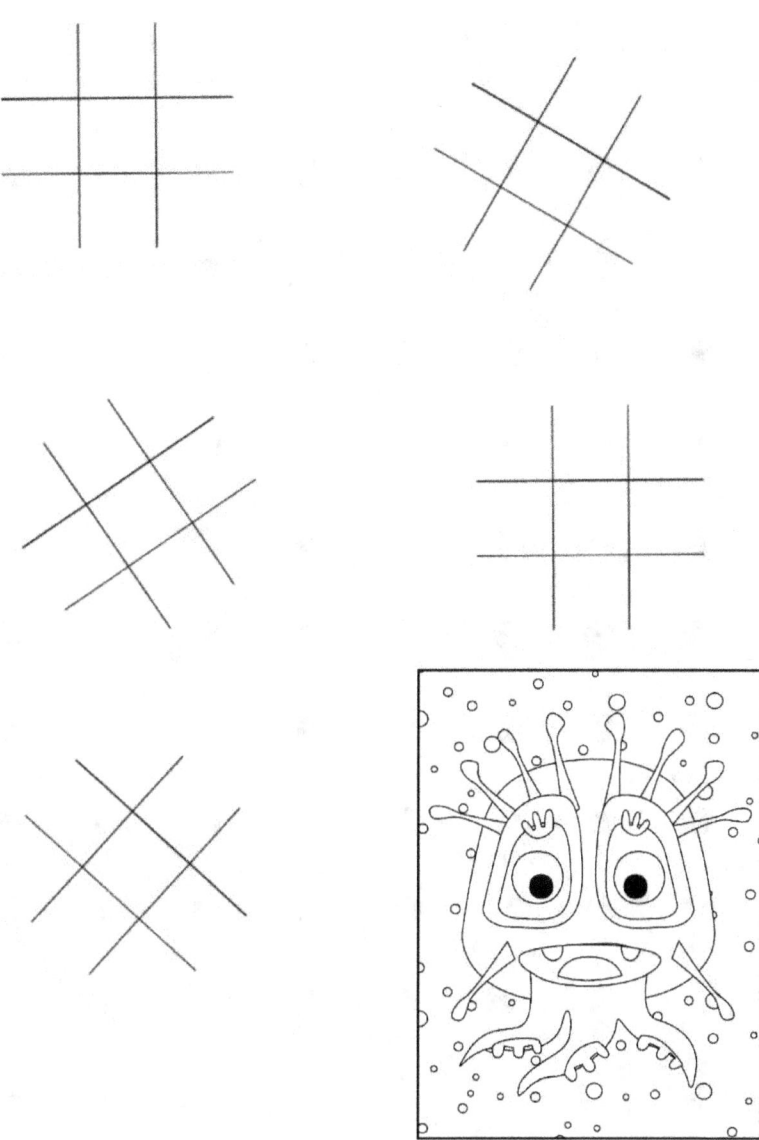

The Dot Game

Take turns connecting the dots until you make a square. Put your initials in each square. At the end, the person with the most squares win.

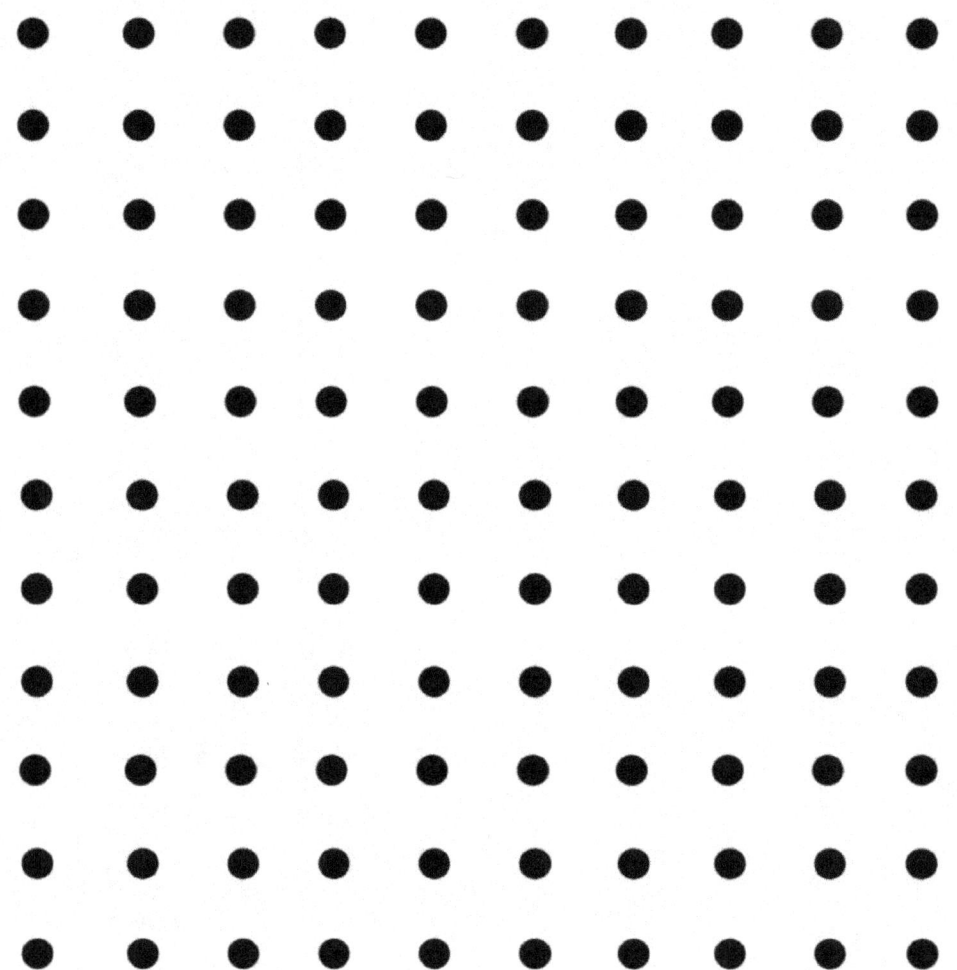

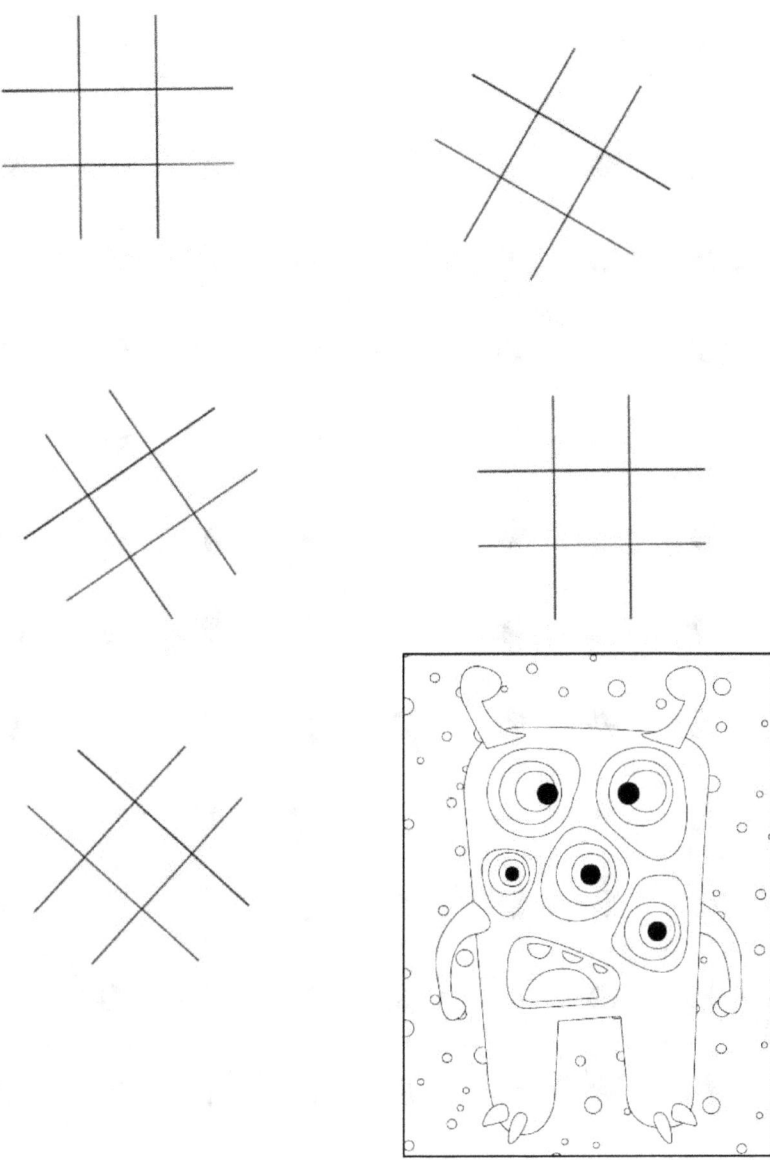

The Dot Game

Take turns connecting the dots until you make a square. Put your initials in each square. At the end, the person with the most squares win.

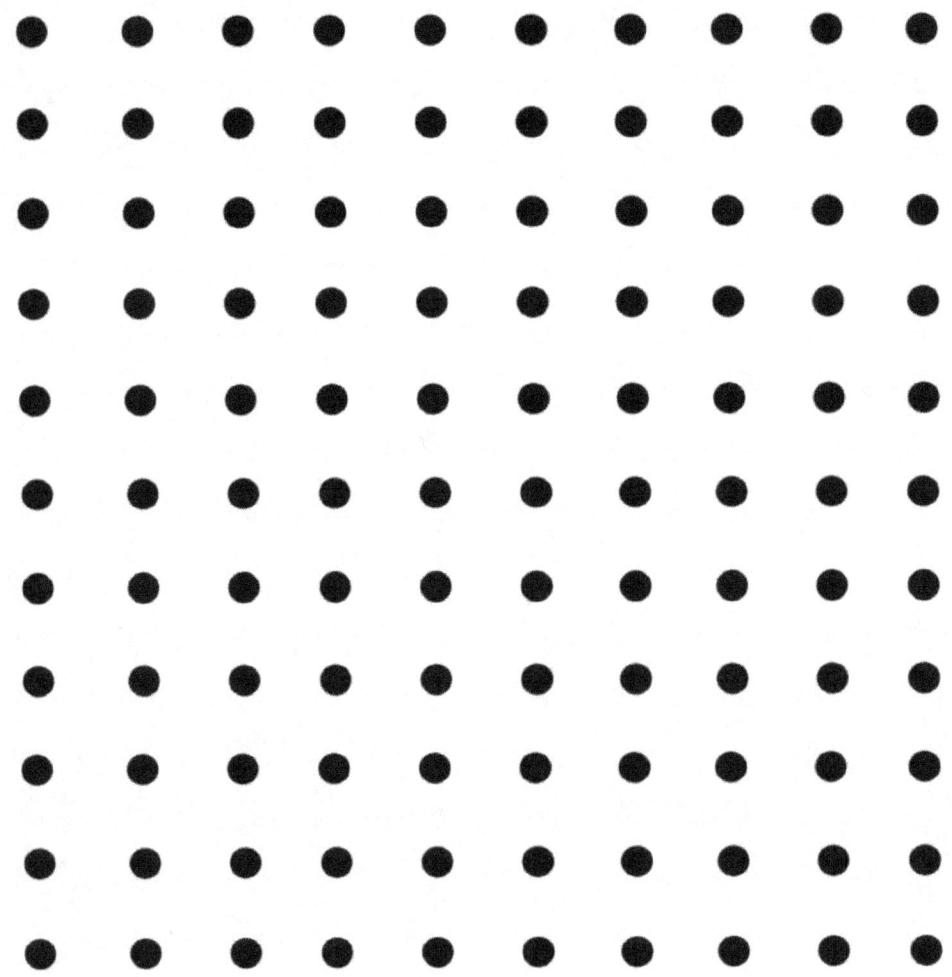

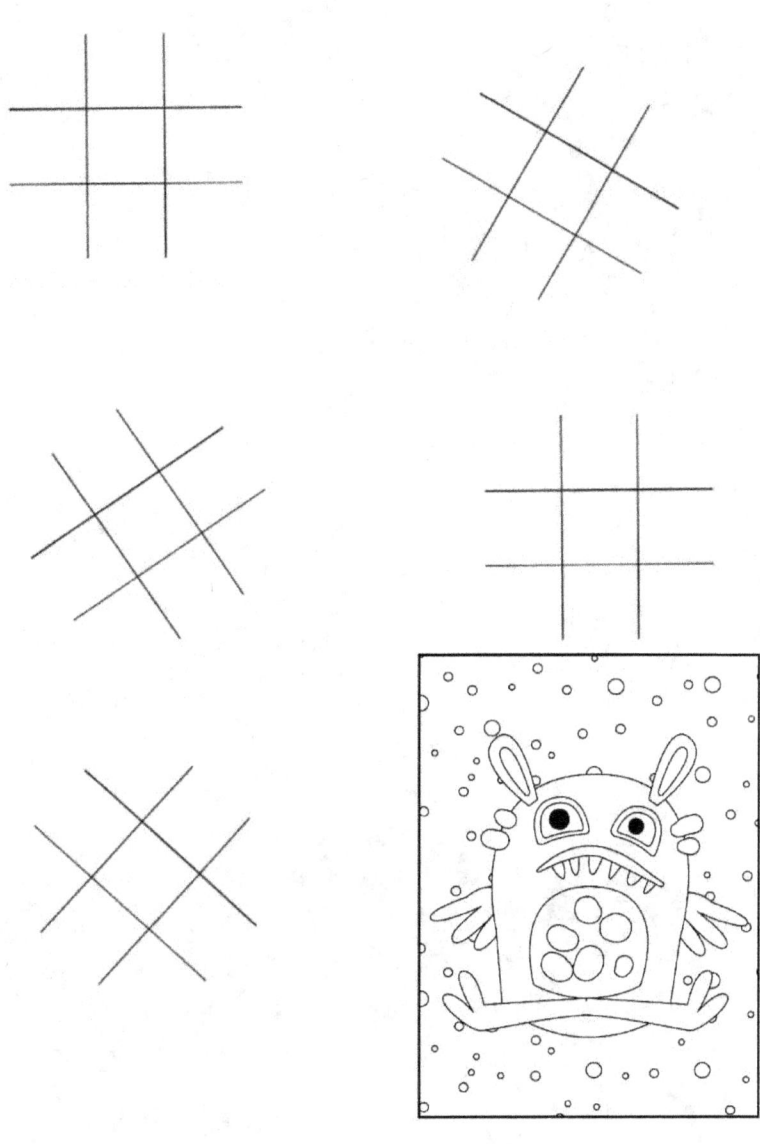

THE AMAZINGLY Fun Jumbo Activity BOOK FOR KIDS

Crossword Puzzles, Mazes, Color by Numbers, Wordsearch, Spot the Difference, Tracing, Unscramble the Words, Connect the Dots, Identify Shapes, Matching, and More Fun Stuff

AN AWARD-WINNING PRINCIPAL OF THE YEAR

DR. MELISSA CAUDLE

Cursive Beginning HANDWRITING WORKBOOK
FOR 2nd – 6th Grade

The Big Coloring Book to Learn Upper and Lowercase Cursive Writing that Includes the Alphabet, Seasons, Months, Numbers, Names, Short Words, & Sentences

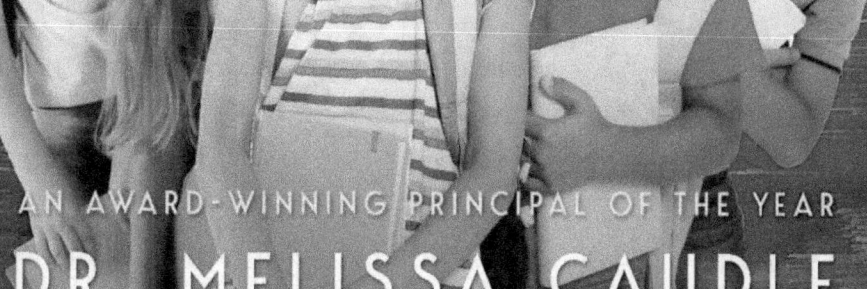

AN AWARD-WINNING PRINCIPAL OF THE YEAR
DR. MELISSA CAUDLE

CROSSWORD PUZZLES

HAVING FUN INCREASING VOCABULARY FOR BOYS AND GIRLS

Volume 1

For KIDS 7 & UP

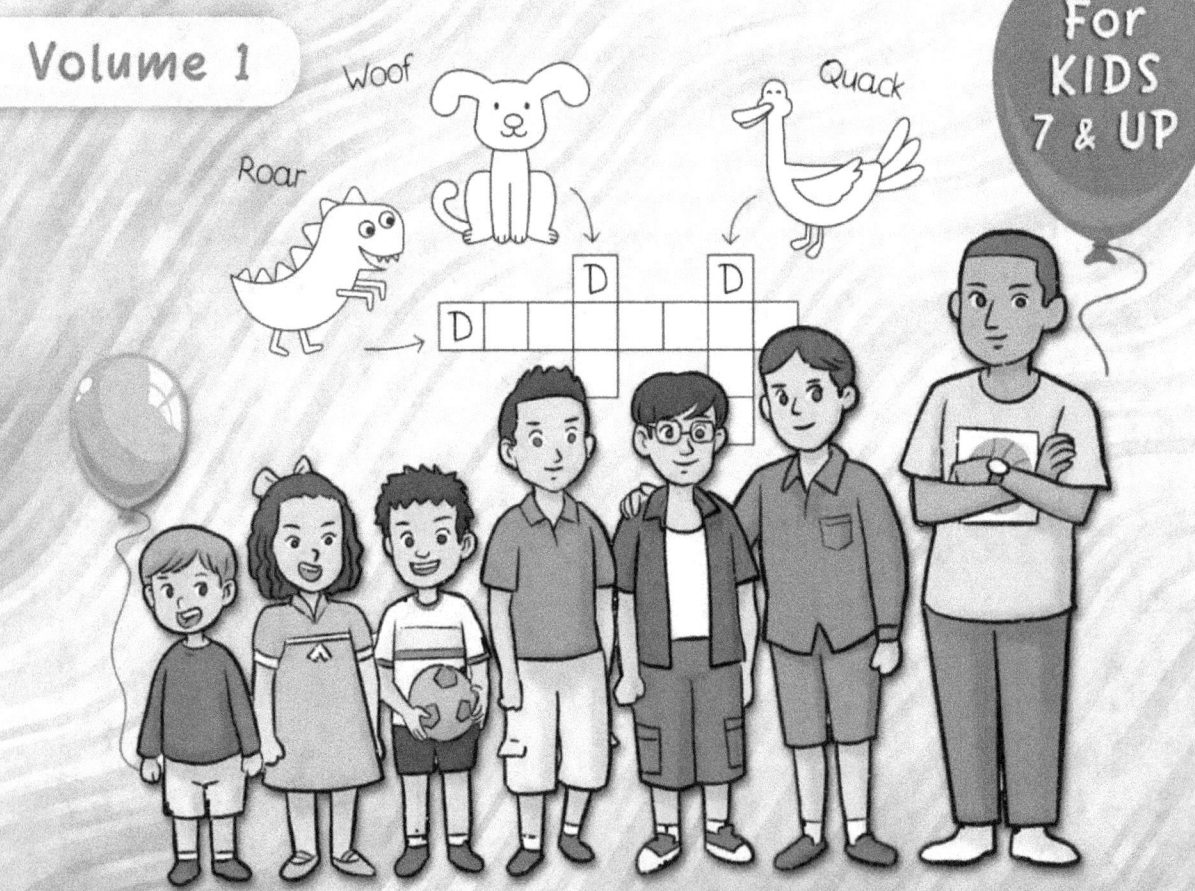

FROM BESTSELLING AUTHOR AND AWARD-WINNING PRINCIPAL OF THE YEAR

DR. MELISSA CAUDLE

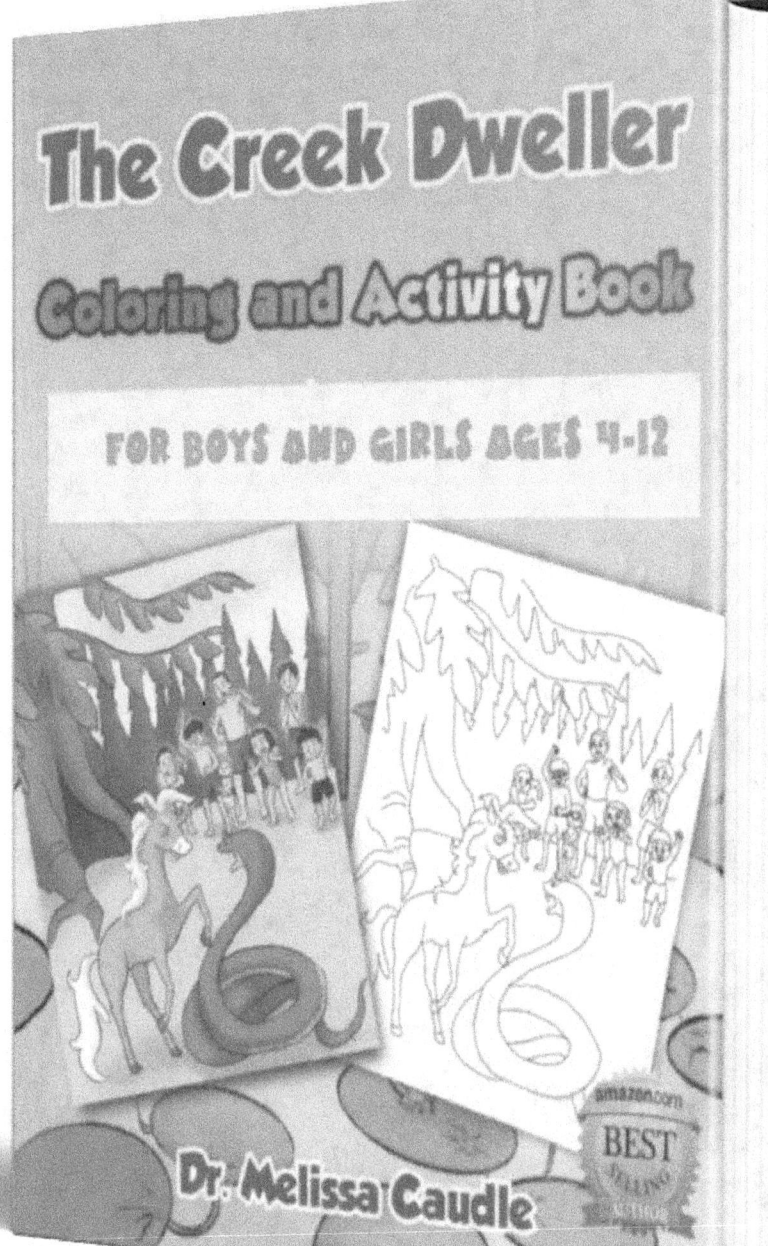

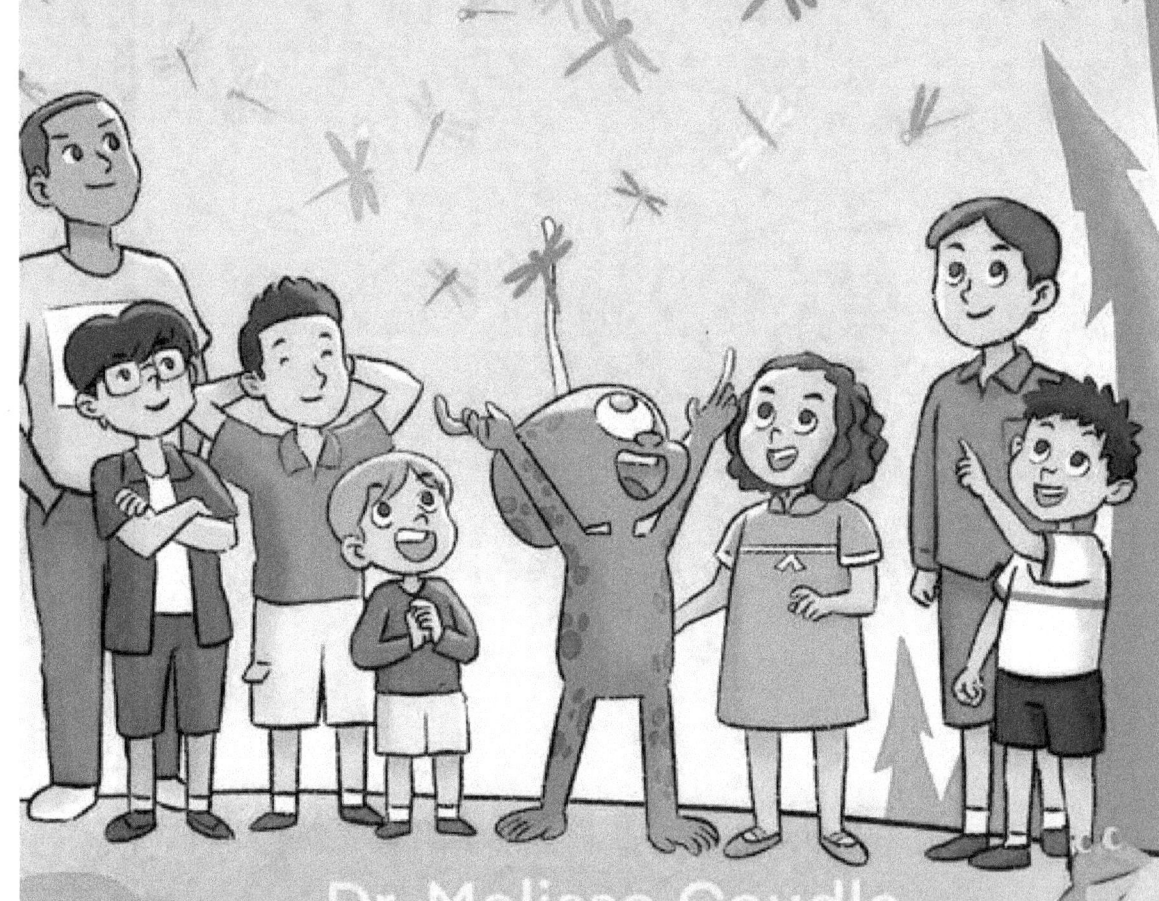

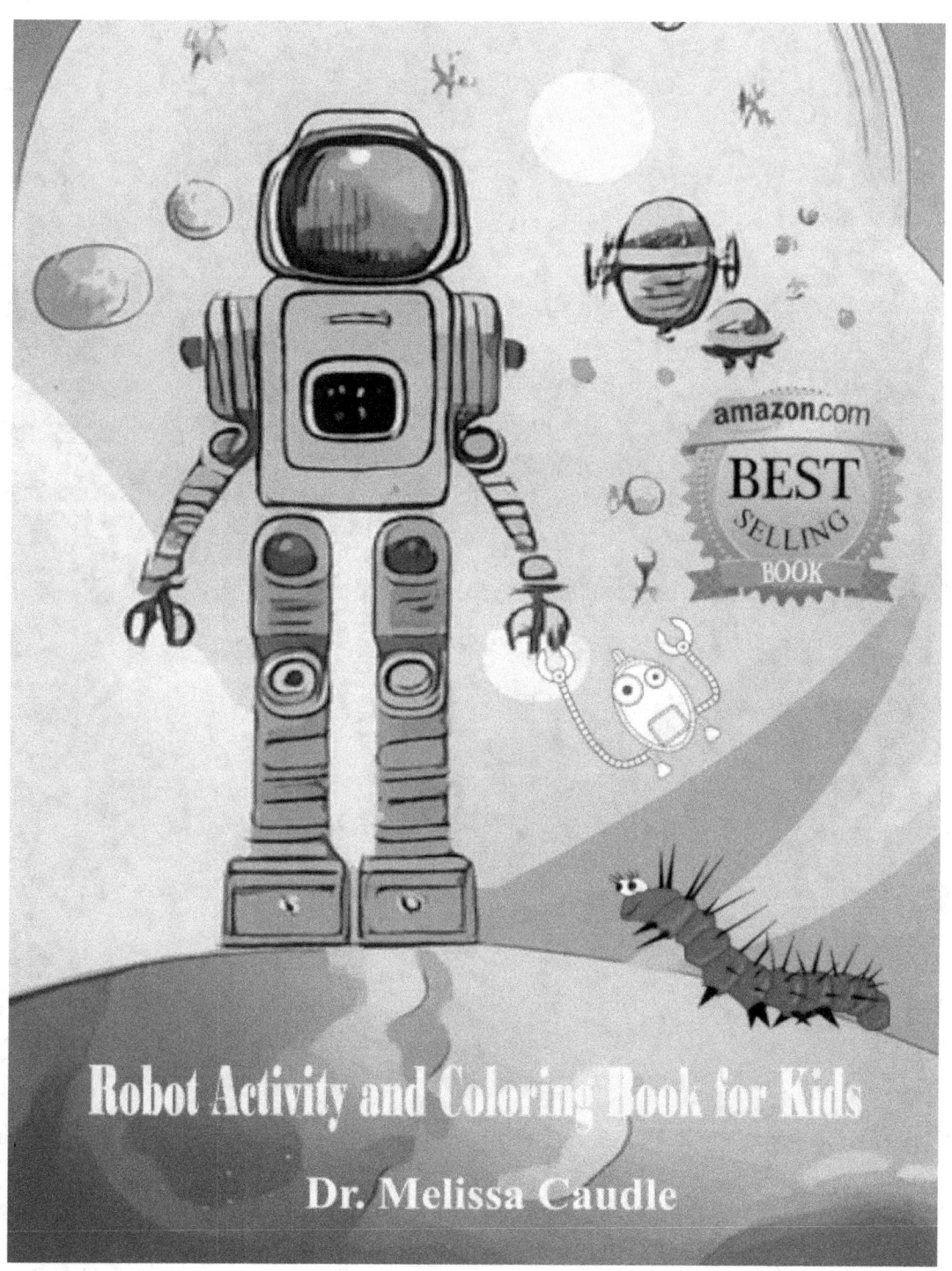

#1 Best Seller

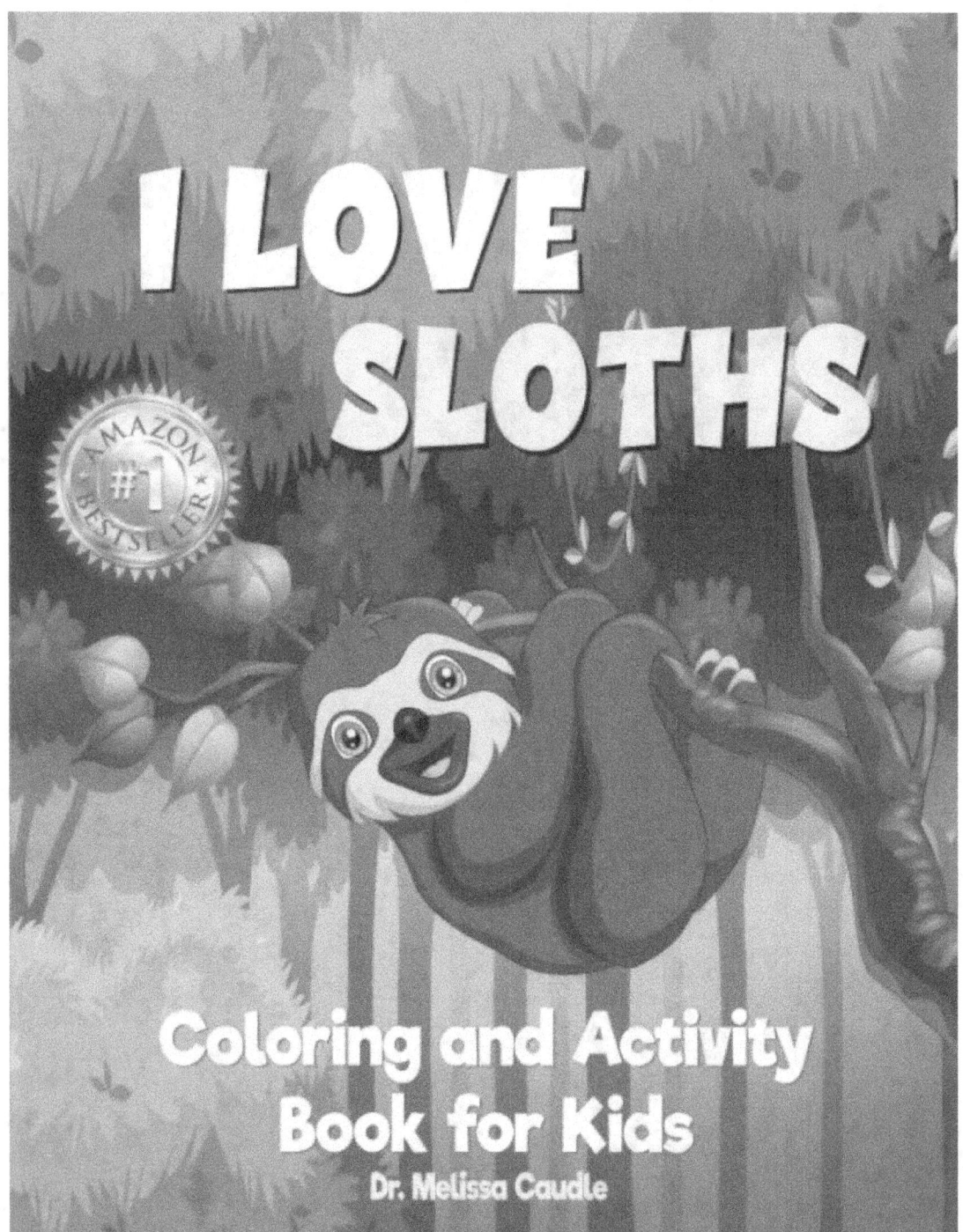

#1 Best Seller

Happy Holidays

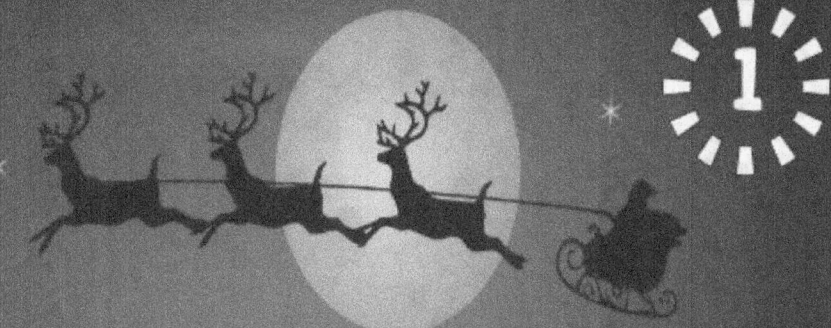

ACTIVITY & COLORING BOOK FOR KIDS

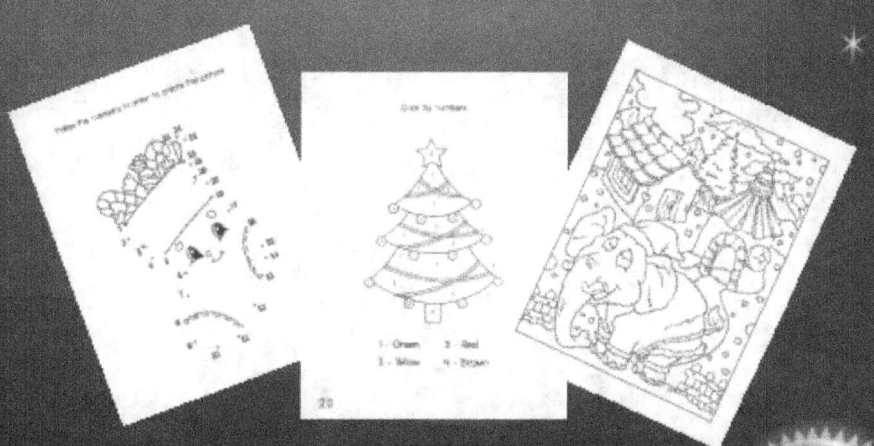

Dr. Melissa Caudle

#1 Best Seller

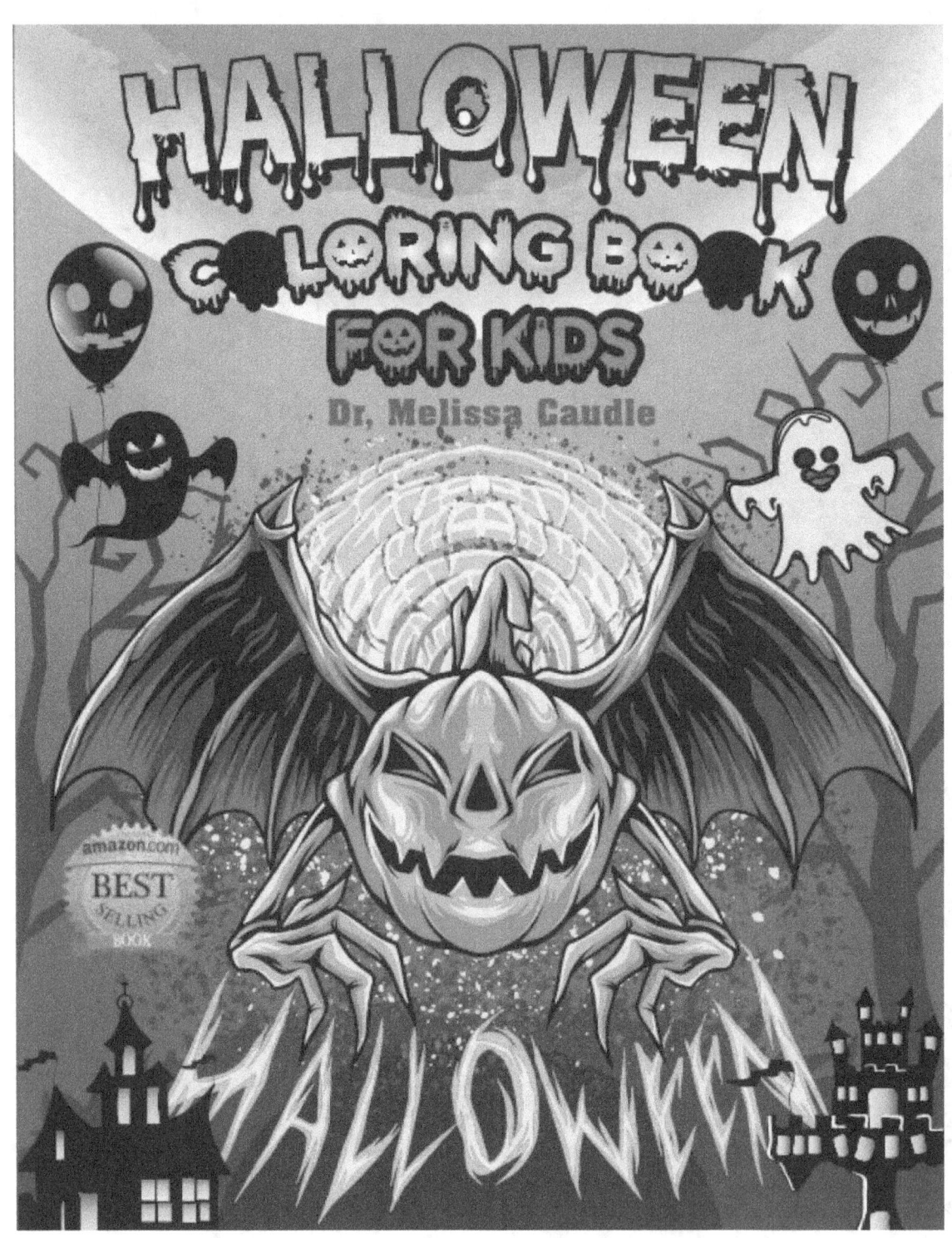

#1 Best Seller

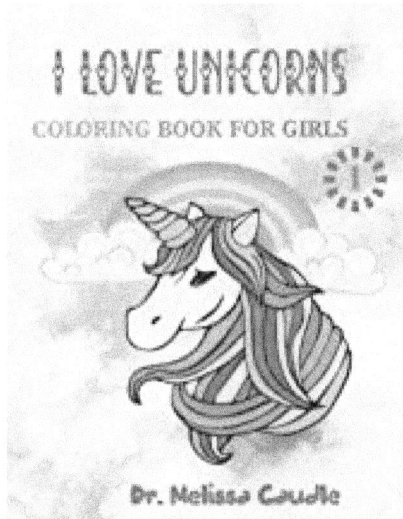
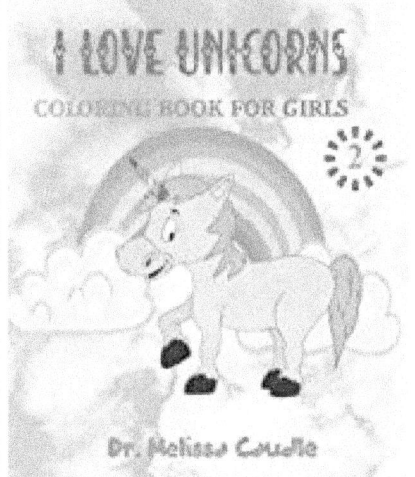
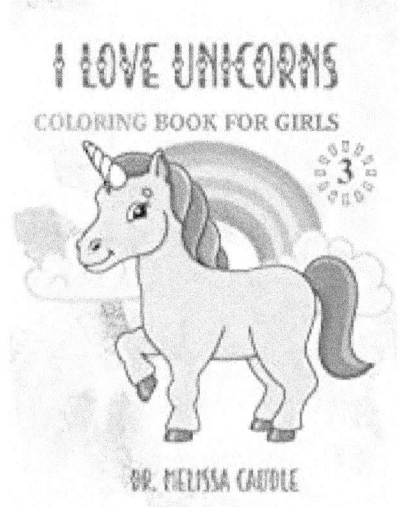
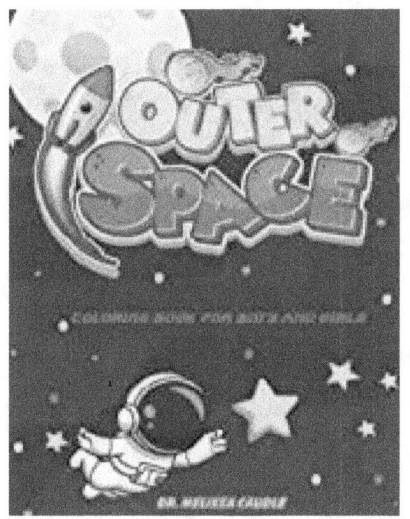
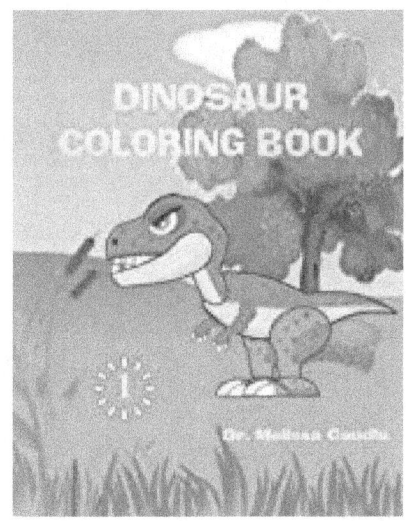
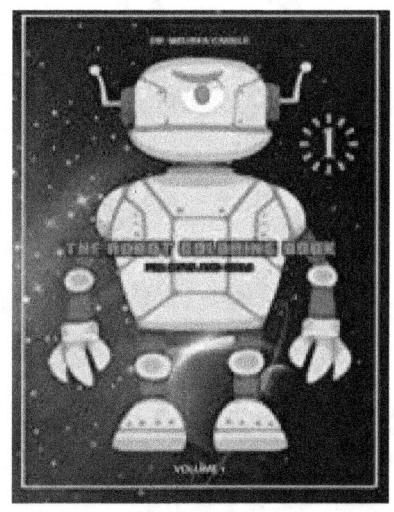
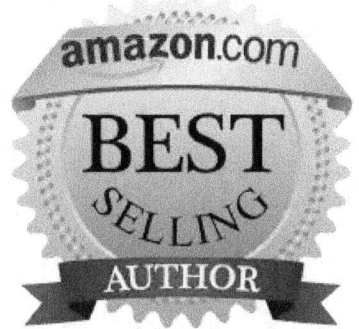